ABRAHAM: FRIEND OF GOD

The *Character and Charisma* series introduces us to people in the Bible and shows how their lives have much to teach us today. All the authors in the series use their communication skills to lead us through the biblical record and apply its encouragements and challenges to our lives today. Every volume contains an *Index of Life Issues* to enhance its usefulness in reference and application.

Other books in the series:

CHARACTER AND CHARISMA SERIES

Abraham
Friend of God

CLELAND THOM

KINGSWAY PUBLICATIONS
EASTBOURNE

Unless otherwise indicated, biblical quotations are
from the New International Version © 1973, 1978, 1984
by the International Bible Society.

ISBN 0 85476 896 3

Published by
KINGSWAY PUBLICATIONS
Lottbridge Drove, Eastbourne, BN23 6NT, England.
Email: books@kingsway.co.uk

Designed and produced for the publishers by
Bookprint Creative Services, P.O. Box 827, BN21 3YJ, England.
Printed in Great Britain.

Contents

This book is dedicated to my father-in-law John Barr, another of God's friends, who went to be with the Lord the day that this book was finally completed.

Acknowledgements

There's a man like Abraham who lives in Essex. His name is John Martin. You probably won't have heard of him. But those of us who know him will understand why I compare him with Abraham, the character in this book. His life has been a pilgrimage of friendship with God, and still is, as he goes around faithfully preaching the word, serving the churches and caring for his wife Joan, who is none too well. He has not always had it easy. But real friends of God never do.

John gave me such a lot of help with this book. In fact I was ready to give up when he stepped in and gave me much-needed focus and clarity about Abraham being God's friend. It probably never occurred to him that he was able to do so because he was one of God's friends too.

I also need to give a huge thank you to God himself for this book. For he performed a miracle, which enabled me to finish it. Halfway through writing it I changed computers, and the hard disk of my original PC was mistakenly erased. All my work was destroyed. And, like a fool, I did not have any back-up. I never backed up (although I always do now . . .). Some friends and I prayed about it and a week later, the lost manuscript mysteriously appeared on a floppy disk that I found in my loft. How it got there I will never know. (Do angels download floppy disks? Why not?) And the work was complete, right up to the half-sentence I had completed before being interrupted by a phone call. A miracle – that's what I call it.

Help came from other sources too. Writing a book like this requires a lot of research and picking the brains of people who understand the Old Testament far better than I ever will. So I have drawn on many books for information. Among them are *Genesis* by W. H. Griffith Thomas, *The Holy Land and the Bible* by Cunningham Geike, the *Tyndale New Bible Dictionary*, the *Royal Tombs of Ur* by the McClung Museum, *The Beginning of Faith* by Ray C. Stedman and the *Matthew Henry Bible Commentary*.

Abraham was a man who was constantly on the move. So it seemed appropriate that almost all of this book was written while I was on the move – on buses, trains and tubes. In fact the whole of Chapter 5 was written when my train broke down for almost two hours one evening. So I also need to thank London Underground, London Buses, Connex South Central and Great Eastern Railways, whose delays provided extended opportunities to write!

You will notice as you read on that I have taken standpoints on issues where the Scriptures are not completely clear. Was Abraham Terah's oldest son, or his youngest? Did he first encounter God in Ur or Haran? Things like this can be argued both ways, so please forgive me if my views differ from yours. But it is in the nature of writing narrative that such decisions must be made. I hope those decisions will not stop you from discovering a deeper friendship with God. After all, that is what this book is about.

Preface

I can still remember my first day at school, venturing out alone into a large, noisy world for the first time, wearing an out-sized blazer. My mum met me at the school gate at the end of the afternoon, and I can remember her words very clearly. 'Hallo, dear! Did you make any friends?' I didn't, not on that first day. It was too bewildering for that. They came later. There was David, Paul and Murray, to name but a few. I still speak to Murray, 41 years on. He lives in Australia now. Over the years I have made some brilliant friends, both in church and outside it. My wife Rachael is the best friend I have ever had.

Friends are cheap these days. We tend to treat them like disposable nappies and chuck them out when things get messy. How sad.

I used to think that I had a friendship with God. That was before I began researching and writing this book. Then I started to discover the depth of relationship that Abraham had with God, and what he went through to achieve it. I realised that I had scarcely begun.

God loves to make friends. That's why he created us. He placed Adam and Eve in the Garden of Eden and called in for a chat every evening. That's what friends do. But sadly, he does

9

not find many friends who are loyal, devoted and prepared to change to become the type of people he feels comfortable with. Most of us either have a working relationship with God, or treat him like the AA – a fourth emergency service, to call on when things go wrong.

Abraham became one of God's friends. In fact he is the only man in the Bible given the honour of being called a friend of God. To this day, Arabs still refer to him as El Khalil, or Friend of God. We know of at least nine times when God appeared to him, in different ways and in different places, and he took steps to develop their friendship in some way every time. Every meeting counted.

I suggest you read Genesis chapters 11 through to 25 before you continue with this book. You will discover that this relationship did not come easily for Abraham. It evolved through years of mistakes, failures, trials and pain. But he got there in the end, emerging as a man with whom God was able to share his heart.

God wants that type of friendship with each of us. Sadly, we are not all prepared to pay the price. Am I? I'm still not sure. Hopefully this book will give you a glimpse of the relationship that it is possible to have with God. I hope Abraham will inspire you in the way he has inspired me. Quite simply, if we can find the friendship with God that he had, our lives will never be the same again.

1

A Friendship Begins

The atmosphere was chilling. You could almost touch the fear. Carefully, slowly, the wooden coffin was carried on an ox-drawn carriage down a steep slope towards the underground burial chamber. Behind it, musicians strummed solemn melodies on their harps and lyres. Maidservants wearing brightly coloured clothes and head-dresses adorned with price-less gems wept as they made their way down the narrow earthen path. Stony-faced soldiers marched in step behind them, their eyes fixed straight ahead, unblinking. Menservants fussed around the carriage, trying to keep it on course.

After a while, the 20-strong procession arrived in the burial chamber. Some members of the party gasped in amazement as they gazed around the ornately decorated tomb. It was a treasure trove. Chests full of gold, silver and precious gems twinkled and blinked in the light from a number of lanterns. Metal tools and weapons were laid out on tables ready to use, along with cosmetics, clothes and other personal belongings.

The grandly dressed high priest offered prayers to the gods Nanna and Sin and then there were muffled cries as workmen arrived, carrying mud bricks and plaster. Quickly and silently they bricked up the chamber entrance from floor to ceiling and

11

when their work was finished they made their way back up the steep shaft and into the temple courts.

The 20 men and women inside the tomb glanced at each other. Some muttered farewells. Others wailed. And then, following a barked command from a high-ranking soldier, they each raised a small clay cup to their lips with frightening precision and swallowed the contents with one gulp. Minutes later they were dead, ready to serve their queen in the next world.

Outside the temple, a crowd stood with heads bowed in the scorching sunshine.

Inside, in a room high above the ground, a temple prostitute screamed as the high priest engaged in sordid fertility rites.

'The queen will be missed,' the old man muttered to his three middle-aged sons as they made their way through the thronging crowds to their two-storey house in the lavish Sumerian city of Ur. The sons didn't reply. Ignoring their silence, the old man pressed on: 'They used one of my statues in the burial chamber! Now that's an honour, isn't it?'

One of the sons broke the silence. 'Honour?' exclaimed Abram. 'How can there be any honour in making an idol to the god Nanna? You should worship Yahweh, the God of Noah, our forefather. He is the only true God. I have seen his glory!' Terah, Abram's father, chuckled mockingly to himself but didn't reply.

The four men arrived back at their comfortable, flat-roofed house, which backed onto several acres of farmland that their family had owned for decades, and went inside to escape the intense 110-degree heat. Sarai, Abram's wife, bowed to her husband and went to prepare some food. She was a beautiful, fair-skinned woman, but her eyes conveyed a deep sadness – the pain of being subject to one of the worst stigmas that could afflict a woman: barrenness. Only her husband and God himself knew the agonies that tormented her heart, and the tears that she shed in secret after being mocked and ridiculed for many years by other women in the town.

Later that night Abram and the rest of his father's household ate a tasty meal of lamb, taken from the pastures and killed that day, accompanied by home-made bread and fresh vegetables grown in the family's lush fields near the River Euphrates.

Outside, the city pulsated to the sound of drunkenness and wild orgies. Mourning had turned to celebration for the worshippers of Nanna.

* * *

Like many of us, Abram didn't exactly have a godly start in life. Quite the opposite, in fact. His father Terah is described in Joshua 24:2 as an idolater, and Jewish tradition refers to him as a maker of idols. Abram probably worshipped them himself when he was young.

By the time Abram was born, God's people – all descendants of Noah and his three sons Shem, Ham and Japheth – had begun to turn away from the one true God to worship idols. Abram was, it seems, one of the few people who remained true to their faith, and history suggests that this caused considerable tension.

The Jewish Book of Jubilees describes how Shem's descendant Eber, the founder of the Hebrew race, was burned to death trying to save some 'images of the gods' from a house that Abram had set on fire. If this legend is true, it seems that there was very real conflict between the Hebrews who wanted to worship God and those who did not.

This conflict certainly affected Abram's family. His father Terah's very name was connected with the moon gods Nanna and Sin who ruled the ancient city of Ur. But somehow Abram managed to discover a relationship with the one true God. His name, which means 'the Father is exalted', certainly turned out to be prophetic. He went on to father a child, a nation and a faith. And he managed to discover the beginnings of a friendship with his heavenly Father, despite the temptations that surrounded him in that wicked city.

We do not know when or how Abram began his friendship with Yahweh. It is likely that he heard about him through stories passed down by word of mouth over the generations by his ancestors. The Bible does not tell us. Maybe God revealed himself to him, through his creation (Psalm 19) or through Abram's conscience (Romans 1:18–20). Or perhaps Abram turned to comforts like money, education and false religions to cope with the deaths of his mother and brother, but found them to be lacking and developed a hunger for the true God instead? We can only speculate. But what is certain is that Abram came to know God in a deeply personal way that none of his ancestors had done since the day Adam and Eve were banished from the Garden of Eden. He got to know him as a God who was just, righteous and wise. He discovered him to be eternal, good and merciful and yet a God who would pass judgement on sin, on nations and indeed on all of mankind. He also found him to be an approachable friend, just as Adam and Eve had done before they spoiled everything through their sin.

It seems that his first encounter with God came while he was living in Ur. Stephen, talking to the Sanhedrin centuries later (Acts 7:2), said, 'The God of glory appeared to our father Abraham while he was still in Mesopotamia, before he lived in Haran.' We don't know what form this glory took. But it seems clear that God broke into the life of a man who had probably been worshipping the moon and kneeling before idols up to then. And the encounter changed his life.

There is some debate about Abram's first encounter with God. Some people think it took place in Haran since it is recounted in Genesis 12:1, *after* he left Ur. But this part of

Genesis is not a chronological account. Genesis 12:1 says, 'The Lord *had* said to Abram . . .' The use of the past tense indicates that the promise that followed had been given earlier – in Ur. This thinking is born out in Stephen's speech.

Abram was brought up in Ur, a beautiful but thoroughly corrupt city in Mesopotamia. The word Mesopotamia means 'the land between' and that is what it was – a city situated between the Tigris and Euphrates rivers. The River Euphrates came right up to the massive city walls, which were so wide that children used to run along the top. Most of it now lies in Iraq.

Ur was one of the first settlements to be established in the region and was located on the border of the al-Hajar desert, just south of the Euphrates on the banks of the life-giving river. It was probably founded around 500 years before Abram was born and is now known as Tell el-Mugayyar, 14 km west of Nasiriyeh.

Ur was advanced and sophisticated, a place of influence and culture, a centre of science, technology and art. It had its own libraries, schools, a university and legal system. Its position by the river, with access to the Persian Gulf, helped it grow into a wealthy, lavish city, with multi-storied houses fitted with lava-tories, kitchens and even their own private chapels. It was fiercely independent, more like a mini-nation than a city. It had its own armies and frequently went to war with other cities, especially to fight over the region's scarce water supplies. It was governed by a king, but because the state and religion were closely intertwined, prosperity depended on the god Nanna, who is believed to have owned and ruled the city with a corrupt regime of rituals, sacrifices and immorality.

Abram was probably the eldest in his family, although many commentators believe he was the youngest. For although Abram is named first in the list of the three brothers in Genesis

11:26, he is named last in the family genealogy in 1 Chronicles 1:5–28. Some people, myself included, believe that the reference in Genesis indicates Abram's importance in the family, whereas the one in Chronicles indicates the order of births. If this is the case, he was not the only youngest son to be used mightily by God. Jacob, Joseph and David would continue the tradition.

Abram and his two brothers were all descendants of Noah's son Shem and were brought up by their idolatrous father in the demon-worshipping environment of Ur. They would have gone to the schools that were attached to the temple and probably accompanied their father on his regular visits there to sing hymns and offer prayers and sacrifices to Nanna.

Of their mother we know nothing. She probably died when Abram was young. All we can piece together about their family is that Abram's brother Haran died while he still lived in Ur (Genesis 11:28). So he was not able to accompany his son Lot (Abram's nephew) and the rest of the family on their pilgrimage into Canaan. Neither did Abram's brother Nahor and his wife Milcah, although they did settle in Haran later.

Abram's wife Sarai was ten years younger than him, and was also his half-sister (inter-marrying was not uncommon during this period of Bible history). Genesis 20:12 tells us that Sarai was the daughter of Abram's father but not his mother. We do not know who her mother was. In fact Moses, in writing Genesis, misses out all kinds of facts that I wish he had included. He does not tell us where Terah, or indeed Abram, was born. But this is probably because Moses was not trying to put together a factual historical account. He was more interested in recording how God worked in the lives of different people.

Nanna was the Sumerian name of the moon god. He was depicted as a fierce young bull, with thick horns and perfect limbs and was the first of the visible gods in that region. Others, like the gods of the air and of the life force in the water, were invisible and could only be sensed, not seen. Nanna was accompanied by the Babylonian moon god Sin. They were the chief deities, but there were thousands of lesser gods beneath them. The temple high priest, chosen from the royal family, was viewed as Sin's spouse. The moon god had different names referring to different phases of the moon. Sin represented the crescent moon, Nanna the full moon, and Asimbabbar the beginning of the lunar cycle.

Ur, like other towns in the region, had its own temple, or ziggurat – a 62 x 43 metre tower that was meant to form a link between heaven and earth. It was built around 2100 BC and was a large, pyramid-shaped structure made of mud bricks cemented with bitumen, with between three and seven terraced levels leading up ramps to the temple at the top. It was beautifully decorated with pillars and other ornaments and was used as a watchtower where worshippers studied the moon and other celestial phenomena. It was similar in many ways to the Tower of Babel. Ur's temple dominated the city and was the centre of religion and learning. It is still the best preserved ziggurat ruin and can be visited today.

In Abram's day, most people believed that the gods Nanna and Sin would either be angry and punish you or would be pleased and reward you. It was the job of the temple priests and priestesses to dictate to the people what the gods wanted, and the worshippers dutifully carried out their wishes. This made the priests and priestesses as powerful as kings. And they were thoroughly corrupt. Whatever they demanded from the people to appease the gods, they inevitably received. Every woman in the city had to serve as a temple prostitute at some time in her life. It is unlikely that Abram's wife Sarai escaped this indignity.[1] And yet from this environment of wickedness, sexual immorality and corruption came a man who became the first in history to be called God's friend; a man who fathered a nation of millions of people who worshipped the only true God; a man who would be a blessing to people everywhere; a man who remains an awesome example of a fearless religious reformer who was prepared to put his faith and relationship with God before everything and everybody. And yet a man who made his mistakes and had his struggles, just as we do.

Abram was also someone who broke out of his family tradition, his culture and his upbringing to pioneer a people and a faith that have both survived thousands of years. He was courageous enough to reject the evil gods worshipped by his generation and the human sacrificial system that went with them, and take huge risks for God.

Maybe we can be courageous enough to follow him and go through the pain barriers needed to become a real friend of God like he did.

If I were asked to draw up an action plan for the upbringing of a future leader of God's people, I would read all the best books on Christian parenting and probably come up with something like this:

1. Find a God-fearing, gifted, stable, church-going couple to be his parents.
2. Make sure he grew up in a good Christian environment.
3. Provide him with the best Christian education.
4. Protect him in every way from the occult, false teaching and immorality.

---

[1] Henry H. Halley, *Halley's Bible Handbook* (Zondervan, 1961), p.95.

And yet when God drew up the plan for Abram's life, he broke all our rules. To our way of thinking, Abram had the worst possible start to life: a godless father, an evil environment, and exposure to idols, false gods and immorality almost every day.

It just goes to show that God can use us, no matter what our past has been like. But this cuts both ways. Because he is the God of redemption and new starts, none of us can blame our parents, our environment, our education or anything else for the way we are. This redemption process does away with the excuses that encourage us to blame everybody and everything else for our behaviour. I remember once complaining to God, 'I'm sure I would find it easier to obey you if I'd had a Christian upbringing.' And he replied, 'If you're a new creation, you can't say that any more. If your heart is eager to obey me, then there's nothing in your past, present or future that will ever stop you doing so. But if your heart is divided, you'll always be looking for an excuse.' Although the blood of Jesus covers my sin, it doesn't cover my excuses.

I remember once going to see Alan, a Christian friend of mine, full of woeful tales about my terrible past and how it was messing up my life. And he said, 'You're what I call a filing cabinet Christian. You drag a filing cabinet of past hurts around behind you and use them as excuses. Why don't you leave it at the cross and get on with life?' Tough advice – but true. And he is still my friend!

Abram was able to succeed for God and become a man who was later judged by history as being God's friend (2 Chronicles 20:7; Isaiah 41:8; James 2:23) – the only man in Scripture to receive this acclaim. And if he was able to do this, despite his ungodly start to life, then we can do the same. Nowhere do we read of him complaining to God about his terrible father or his godless upbringing. All we read about is a man who put his past behind him and got on with the job God called him to. An example for all of us.

*   *   *

'But I'm too old to move.' Terah's eyes blazed with anger at his son.

'Well, we're going,' replied Abram. 'I've decided.'

'What, all of you?'

'Well no, not all of us. But myself, Sarai, Lot and all our servants.'

'And where are you going?' demanded Terah angrily.

Abram paused. He was dreading his father asking him that question. 'Well, I don't know yet,' he said cautiously. 'But I know that God will show us.' Terah cursed at the mere mention of the name. Abram ignored him and carried on. 'He has appeared to me and told me we must leave, so the matter is settled. You can come with us if you want to, or you can stay here in Ur. It's up to you.'

'But you're all I have!' cried Terah. 'Who will look after me as I get older? I'm becoming too old to work.'

'Then you'd better come with us,' said Abram uneasily, remembering God's word – 'leave your father's household'. He carried on, hesitantly, wondering if he was making a big mistake: 'There will always be a place for you. We will look after you. But you must decide quickly. I want to move within the next month.'

Sometime later, neighbours came out into the streets to watch Terah, Abram and their family leave their home for the last time. The preceding weeks had been hectic – a house and land to sell, furniture and other goods to dispose of, arrangements to be made. But eventually moving day arrived and this Hebrew family joined a camel caravan and headed north-west into the sandy, blistering unknown.

*   *   *

Have you ever prayed a prayer that you wish you'd never prayed? My wife and I did just that, soon after we were married. Consumed with zeal to serve the Lord, and desperate to keep our cutting edge, we told him, 'Lord, we pray that we never grow comfortable or settle down.'

God took us at our word. Things have been neither comfortable nor settled ever since! We have moved house nine times in fourteen years. For us, life has been a roller-coaster, with some amazing highs, some desperate lows and some intriguing adventures of faith and encounters with God along the way. Sometimes I wish I'd never prayed that prayer. But most of the time I'm glad I did. For those ups and downs and those times of pain and uncertainty have helped me develop a trust and a relationship with God that I would never have had otherwise.

I hate moving house. The endless packing and humping boxes and furniture drives me to distraction, although I have to admit that it is always exciting, moving somewhere new. But at least when I have moved, I have known where I was going! Abram didn't.

For him, the sacrifices must have been enormous. He left a life of comfort and luxury for one where there were no financial certainties. He left the security of the town where he had lived all his life for an unknown destination. He put his entire future into God's hands without any guarantees. It could have all gone wrong, especially as his friendship with God was in its infancy and he did not have years of experience to draw on. But he made the break and went. In doing so he became what the Hebrew language calls a *ger*. Translated, that means 'a resident alien'. This is what we should all aspire to be. Not just pilgrims, but extra-terrestrials – people who live here on earth but who don't really belong here, because our values, our futures and our citizenship belong somewhere else. This doesn't just apply to us as individuals either. It applies to our churches too. We are called to be a community that is always moving on, that never settles, that is always looking for new horizons and fresh challenges. If we ever lose that pilgrim mentality, then all we end up with is lifeless religion.

There come times in all our lives when we have to make the break and move on, like Abram did. This will mean different things to each of us. But God will inevitably challenge us about our priorities and call us to examine whether he is more important than our families, friends, jobs, ambitions and money. Sooner or later we have to plunge into the deep water where only God can catch us. It's a decision that we all have to make if we are going to go the whole way in pursuing a friendship with God. Peter, Andrew, James and John – Jesus' first disciples – had to face it. When Jesus' call came (Matthew 4:18ff) they left their jobs and their families and followed him. Again, there were no guarantees; they did not know where they were going or for how long. They had to walk in faith and trust God. I don't suppose they found it any easier than Abram did. But they went anyway. It was all or nothing, and still is.

It can be hard. But God understands this. That's why Jesus reminded Peter later on, 'No-one who has left home or wife or brothers or parents or children for the sake of the kingdom of God will fail to receive many times as much in this age and, in the age to come, eternal life' (Luke 18:29). Jesus knew that Peter had paid a hefty price to join his band of companions and wanted to reassure him that it would all be worthwhile, both now and in the long run.

Perhaps you have shied away from launching out for God without a lifebelt. Or maybe you've done it and have found the sacrifices too hard to bear. You've given up everything, but seen little or nothing in return. If so, Jesus' promise to Peter will hold good if you are prepared to wait. It did for Abram.

* * *

Months had passed and Abram's group of travellers had journeyed many miles across the vast desert wastes. The servants went at the head of the procession, guiding scores of animals along with sticks, taking extra care with the pregnant ewes and carrying lambs in their arms or on their shoulders. Next came the women, travelling uncomfortably on camels or asses, while Abram and the other men rode up and down the procession to make sure everybody was all right. They had endured months of intense heat by day and bitter cold by night. Months of searching for pastures for the flocks and places to pitch their animal-skin tents. Months of thirst, of fighting off gangs of robbers and wild animals. Months of sandstorms and sudden, terrifying floods. Months of torturously slow progress for mile after aching mile. Abram was weary. And Terah was becoming ill.

Abram had been watching his father closely for several days and was worried about him. He began to doubt the wisdom of bringing an old man on such a long and difficult journey – after all, Terah was over 150 now. Again, God's word given him in Ur came back to mind: 'Leave your father's household'. It was too late to change things now. They were hundreds of miles into their journey. Eventually, Abram decided that they needed a rest.

Later that evening, as the family gathered round the camp-fire for supper, Abram told them, 'I think we need to have a break for a while. We are all tired and father is becoming ill. Haran is only days away. Let's stay there for a time. Then we will be strong enough to continue with our journey.'

There was murmured consent and Abram noticed that his father seemed to show signs of improvement from his illness. He wasn't surprised. Haran was another city like Ur,

dominated by the worship of the moon god Sin. He smiled
wryly and thought to himself, 'At least father will feel at home
there.'

Three days later, they arrived.

*   *   *

Haran was almost exactly halfway between Ur and Canaan in
Syria, situated at the junction of three main trade routes,
including the main roadway from Nineveh to Aleppo. Its name
means 'parched', and it was just that – a place scorched by the
sun. It was spiritually dry too. It was not far from the Turkish
border and was surrounded by a high wall with twelve gates.
For Terah, it must have been home from home. Maybe he liked
it because it reminded him of his dead son, who bore the same
name.

Haran had very close links with Ur, both commercially and
spiritually. The two towns had a great deal in common. They
were both situated on rivers, Haran standing near the banks of
the River Balih. They were both major commercial centres, as
well as being dedicated to the worship of the moon gods. Both
had temples. The temple at Haran had a roof covered with
cedar trees from Lebanon. Haran was well known for its
unusual square and cone-shaped clay houses. These dwellings
were up to five metres high and were cool and comfortable
inside.

Terah had distant family living in Haran. Laban's family
lived there. And the town later became significant to Abram's
descendants – both Isaac and Jacob found their wives there,
and all but one of Jacob's children were born in Haran.
Although Abram's household was always on the move in
Canaan, Haran always remained the nearest thing it had to a
family base.

Abram's stay in Haran certainly was not as brief as he had

intended. Genesis 11:31 tells us that he and his fellow-travellers settled there. Some people believe it was more than 50 years. But it was certainly long enough for them to put down family roots, and accumulate the 'possessions and people' referred to in Genesis 12:5. And Terah never left. He died there, aged 205, a tragic figure whose son left him behind in his pursuit of God.

We do not know why Terah didn't make it to Canaan. Maybe it was family ties. Or his love of false gods. Or tiredness. Or the income he would have received from making idols in a town devoted to idolatry. Whatever the reason, he is a lesson to all of us who are on that pilgrimage of developing a friendship with God. So many of us start well but give up before we finish. As with Terah, family ties, or gods from our past, or tiredness or money make us become settlers. We pitch our tents in Haran, halfway towards our goal, and stay there. We compromise with the natives and enjoy the worldly enticements they offer us. We don't go back, of course. Terah never went back to Ur. But we don't go the distance either. And as a result we fail to enter into the full riches of God and are content to stay put and impress others with stale stories about the journey so far. We forget to tell them that we aren't actually planning to finish the course.

Abram was a man who went the distance. Even though he settled in Haran for many years, he never lost sight of his goal: to move to the place God would show him. Even at this stage in his journey, he still did not know his final destination. He probably never wanted to remain in Haran for as long as he did. He was the type of character who would have wanted to keep going. But he had to learn other lessons in Haran – the lessons of patience and love. Maybe he knew God's heart well enough to realise that he needed to care for his ageing father, and that his duty in this respect was more important than his journey.

So Abram reminds us of the other side of stopping in our Haran, wherever that may be: sometimes we must. We have no choice. We may sometimes need to 'settle' for a few years to look after our ageing parents, our partners or our young children. In our eagerness to pursue our goals, our ministries and our callings, it's easy to neglect the ones who are closest to us. The rest will probably do us good, and will certainly teach us patience and that loving our families is just as spiritual as church activity in God's eyes. After all, that's all Noah ever did. His whole ministry involved little else than protecting his family and bringing them through God's judgement.

Eventually, though, the time came for Abram to move on. Behind schedule to his own way of thinking, but not too late in God's eternal timescale.

2

A Time of Promise

Abram poked the embers of the fading fire with a stick and drew his cloak tightly round his neck as protection against the bitter desert cold. The silence of the night was almost frightening, the eerie stillness punctuated only by the occasional noises of the animals. The rest of his household had been asleep in their camel-skin tents for a long time. But Abram was still wide awake. Many things were going through his mind. He shivered, sipped a drink and gazed into the clear, black night as he had done a hundred times before. Those stars had always fascinated him.

His household had been on the move again for several weeks following the burial of Terah in Haran. Abram still recoiled in disgust at the memory of the pagan funeral ceremony, with its hymns and prayers to Nanna and the endless bowing to statues. But within weeks of the burial he was preparing to continue with the trip he had started all those years earlier.

This time it had not been a small family who headed into the desert, but a large gathering of people: his family, plus servants and their families whom Abram had acquired in Haran, together with hundreds of sheep, cows and goats. People

27

watched with a mixture of mockery and disbelief as these pilgrims mounted their camels and headed into the wilderness, their destination still unknown.

Abram turned his gaze away from the sky and recollected the words God had spoken to him years earlier, when their friendship first began: 'Leave your country, your people and your father's household and go to the land I will show you.' He pondered over the words. Well, he had certainly left his country – the Chaldees were well and truly behind him and he never intended to go back there. And the same applied to his people. He had not just walked away from his native country but from friends and business associates too. But leaving his father's household . . .

A wolf shrieked raucously in the night, causing the animals to stir again. Abram was distracted from his train of thought for a moment. But then those words came back to him again: 'leave your father's household'. This was the problem. He had not done as God had said and had already reaped the consequences: a long delay in Haran looking after his troublesome father. He scratched his head thoughtfully and looked over to the big tent where his nephew Lot and his wife were sleeping soundly. Leaving his father's household had surely meant leaving Lot behind too. Abram looked up at the stars again and had a feeling that he might continue to regret his decision not to co-operate fully with God's word.

* * *

Travelling light

God was very clear to Abram. He was going on a journey. Not just a physical one, to a different place, but also a pilgrimage of friendship with his heavenly Father. And he would have to travel light. This didn't mean he had a baggage allowance like you have when you check in at the airport. God had other baggage in mind. He knew that other things could hold Abram back from developing a relationship of real depth and quality with him – the same things that can hold us back on our journeys too: our culture, our people, and our father's household. Let's look at them.

1. Culture shock?

God doesn't usually want us to rush off to a foreign land as soon as we become Christians. But he does want us to break free from our culture and follow his culture instead. This means rejecting the world's priorities of ambition, and the worship of money, fame and power. For 1 John 2:15 makes it very clear that we should not love the world or anything in it.

Culture is the most potent force in our lives. It governs what we wear, how we behave, what we eat, what time we go to bed, how we treat others – almost everything we do, in fact. And when we become Christians, God's agenda is to give us a new set of values and new patterns of behaviour. This inevitably causes a clash. At that point, we either allow God to change us, or we opt to remain in our culture, claim it's God's will and never reach our full potential as disciples. It's so easy to say we have become Christians while continuing to live the way we've always done.

Marriage problems are often caused by cultural differences. Our partners may have different ways of doing things, based on their upbringing. They get up early, have high tea and supper, whereas we get up later and have lunch and dinner. They open their Christmas presents on Christmas Eve. We open ours after lunch on Christmas Day. Then we wonder why there are arguments! Neither culture is right or wrong – just different.

Culture can divide churches too. Some people might have

grown up in a formal church culture. Others might have been brought up in a church that was comparatively relaxed. And the problems really begin when each side finds a Bible verse to justify their behaviour and claim that *they* are in God's will. The 'formals' will tell you, 'Everything should be done in a fitting and orderly way' (1 Corinthians 14:40), while the 'informals' will claim, 'Where the Spirit of the Lord is, there is freedom' (2 Corinthians 3:17). A recipe for problems. And in fact both sides are wrong. Neither has understood that their views are based more on their culture than Scripture and that Scripture primarily calls believers to love one another and maintain unity.

Culture is also the cause of racism, one of the most insidious evils in our society. Our insecurity makes us reject anybody who is different from us. Again, we find all kinds of Bible texts to prove that our country's way of doing things is the right way, and in doing so we immediately alienate everybody else. No wonder wars start!

God's challenge to each of us is to break free from all cultural ties, whether they are national, church or family, and enter into the new way of life and thinking that he offers us through Jesus.

When Jesus was on earth he broke just about every cultural rule there was. He spoke to women and even worked with them. He mixed with people outside his class. He was a working-class carpenter, and yet was able to get on easily with both educated Pharisees and prostitutes. He was friendly to the foreigners whom the racists despised. He broke man-made regulations regarding the Sabbath and didn't wash his hands before he ate. He was not bound by tradition, the status quo, philosophies or social rules and conventions.

If you ask God today to show you the areas where you are in the grip of your culture, you might be surprised at what you discover! Abram was able to walk away from an affluent city lifestyle to become a desert nomad. Imagine the changes he had to cope with! But he knew they were essential if he was to reach his goal. And if he coped, then so can we!

2. The people factor

Breaking away from people is something that many Christians are much *too* good at! We have a big circle of friends, but as soon as we become believers we abandon them and build all our relationships around church. There's nothing wrong with having friends in church – it's essential. But forgetting our non-Christian friends shows a lack of integrity and loyalty towards them and also denies them the chance to hear about this new God of ours. I always find it astonishing that so many Christians I know have no non-Christian friends at all.

However, God does want us to break away from unhealthy relationships; from people who might hold us back or lead us into wrong-doing. We are warned in 1 Corinthians 15:33, 'Bad company corrupts good character.' And remember, this was written to Christians. When we become Christians we may have to say no to certain friendships and even long-term lovers. And if we decide to keep in touch, we need to make it clear that we are different now and that there are certain things we won't do any more. If we compromise, we eventually risk losing all that God has given us. We should not be worried about what others think of what we say or do. It's what God thinks that matters.

3. Family fortunes

Families can be a big battleground for Christians, and most people in the Bible faced the same problems we do. Even Jesus was not immune from unhelpful family influences (Matthew 12:48). Matthew tells us, 'Pointing to his disciples, he said,

"Here are my mother and my brothers. For whoever does the will of my Father in heaven is my brother and sister and mother." '

There's nothing wrong with families – God invented them and created us out of them. We are called to love them and to pray for them. The last thing God wants is for us to be like the sects that isolate members from their families. But our loved ones can sometimes hold us back. Almost everyone I know who has decided to be baptised has received a warning not to from some 'helpful' family member. We need to break free from these family ties. And the break must be so clean in our hearts that we 'hate' our families compared with the love we have for God. And the word 'hate' was Jesus' word (Luke 14:26), not mine! It can be hard. But avoiding the issue is even harder in the end, as Abram found with Lot. His nephew was nothing but a problem to him throughout his travels, causing endless trouble because of his double-mindedness and his fascination with sin. Abram paid a high price for ignoring God's command.

* * *

The sky slowly began to turn lighter. Soon the sun would rise from behind the silky sand dunes and splash an awesome array of gold, orange and pink across the heavens. Abram loved the sunrise.

He yawned and broke off a piece of bread. It was stale but he still chewed it hungrily. The promises God had made him back in Ur still burned strongly in his heart: 'I will make you into a great nation and I will bless you; I will make your name great and you will be a blessing. I will bless those who bless you, and whoever curses you I will curse; and all peoples on earth will be blessed through you.'

Abram turned those words over in his mind for the

thousandth time, and still could not work out what they meant. How could he become a nation when he did not even have a land or children of his own, and, given Sarai's barrenness, was never likely to produce an heir? How could his name become great when no one outside Ur and Haran had ever heard of him? And how indeed could all people on the earth be blessed through him, when he had given up all possibility of power and influence when he moved and he still did not have any descendants?

He ate some more bread, washed it down with a few sips of precious water and shook his head in wonder. He was certain that those words were true. And he had acted on them by setting off on his journey, just as God had said. What more could he do? As the sun began to scatter rosey panels of light across the sand, Abram nodded off to sleep, satisfied that if God had made those promises, then the outcome was up to him. He was beginning to learn that friendship with God is all about trust.

*   *   *

Abram was a man who learned that it is important to obey God straight away, decisively and without question. He did not manage it at the first attempt. Had he been that good, he would never have taken Terah and Lot with him on his journey. But he got there in the end. And I am convinced this was the main key to his spiritual success. Even though he probably did not understand God's promises, he launched out on them anyway.

In some ways God's word was very clear. He told Abram to leave Ur and gave him very clear promises for the future. But on the other hand, God was mysteriously vague: he told Abram to go, but didn't say where to! He simply said it was a land 'I will show you'. You often find God is like this with his guidance. He tells you some things, but never everything. There's always an unexplained element to make sure you remain dependent on him. And Abram obeyed as best he could and left everything else to God. Maybe you or I would have 'laid a fleece' (Judges 6:37), asked for a sign, and demanded several other words, plus a few prophecies thrown in, before making a few tentative steps forward. Not Abram. He simply upped and went. Hebrews 11:8 tells us, 'By faith Abraham, when called to go to a place he would later receive as his inheritance, obeyed and went, even though he did not know where he was going.' It shows how clear he was in his relationship with God. He knew without doubt who had spoken to him. And the fact that God said, 'I will' six times when giving him those promises must have helped. If God says 'I will', then he will!

Promises, promises

Let's look at the promises God gave Abram, and how God has kept them over thousands of years. They were not just promises made for the sake of it. They amounted to a contract that was the foundation of a loving friendship between God and one man. They undergirded their relationship, acting as a guarantee that it could never fail.

1. 'I will make you into a great nation'

This promise must have been a mystery to Abram. It could not have made any sense at all. He had become a desert wanderer, alone apart from his family and servants, heading to a country he had never been to. Yet he would become a great nation! And it happened. The Jewish nation was established through him and has proved to be the most durable race ever known to man. It is unique. Every other nation on earth is made up of hundreds of thousands of strains from different family groups. But God's nation began with just one man whose family grew and grew until a whole race was established. As well as occupying their own nation-state of Israel, you will also find Jewish people in many other countries. And you often find that they retain their identity as Jews, while other immigrants eventually become absorbed into the native culture within a generation or two. This would never have happened without God.

The Jewish race is also one of the most ethnically pure – one of the few races able to make such a claim after 4,000 years, undoubtedly due to God's command for them not to inter-marry. Without doubt, God's promise of making Abram into a great nation has been fulfilled, and is still being outworked today among his people. For Abram did not just father a nation. He also, and more importantly, fathered a people of faith. He imparted his lifestyle of faith first of all to the Jewish nation and then to us, God's chosen people, under the new covenant.

2. 'I will bless you'

The Bible tells us that Abram was blessed materially. Genesis 13:2 says that he was wealthy in livestock, silver and gold. And he and his family were blessed in other ways too. His wife Sarai retained her beauty right into old age, to the extent that foreign kings wanted to take her into their harems. God's blessing extended to every area of Abram's life – his health, his safety, nothing was missed out. And that blessing has been passed down to his descendants too. Although the Jews have suffered terrible persecution, they are rarely known as poor people. They have always been powerful in business and have wielded great influence. This is why Hitler hated them. They are still as influential today. Israel, though a tiny nation, has a power on the world stage out of all proportion to its size.

3. 'I will make your name great'

God has certainly made Abram's name a great one. Apart from

Jesus, he is probably the most widely known religious figure on earth. Moses devoted almost a quarter of the book of Genesis to him, and he is referred to 40 times in the Old Testament and 75 times in the New.

Paul chose him (Romans 4) as the finest example of a man who was justified by faith. James referred to him as someone who demonstrated his faith by works (James 2:21–23). The writer of Hebrews devoted more space to him than anybody else when listing the great heroes of faith in chapter 11. The Islamic religion gives him enormous status too, placing him second only to Muhammad. The Koran mentions him 188 times. In fact he is said to be the father of three religions: Christianity, Judaism and Islam.

All this shows that if God decides to give someone profile, nothing can stop him. And if he wants to keep someone under wraps, again nothing can stop him. I often chuckle when I see itinerant ministers desperately trying to promote themselves, spending fortunes on advertising, mailshots and publicity. We should learn from Abram. He did absolutely nothing to promote himself. Quite the opposite, in fact. In leaving Ur he walked out on any possibility of political or religious power and status. But because God was his marketing manager, he became famous – not just for a few years, but for centuries. Jesus said, 'My Father will honour the one who serves me' (John 12:26). We need to avoid self-promotion and let God give us profile if he wants to.

4. 'You will be a blessing'

I once went to the funeral of a dear old lady called Auntie Rose. She was my wife's aunt, a lady who really loved the Lord and, even in her old age, never went out of the house without some tracts in her handbag to give to people she met. People at the funeral said that her name had been really appropriate, because she left a beautiful fragrance of kindness and love wherever she went. She was the type of person Paul had in mind in 2 Corinthians 2:15–16: 'For we are to God the aroma of Christ.' This is what being a blessing is all about. We all leave a fragrance behind us. But is it the sweet smell of encouragement, praise and love, or the revolting stench of gossip, innuendo and criticism?

The hallmark of any Christian is that they should be a blessing to other people. I once met a man called Phil in St James' Park, London. He told me that he had given up everything to preach Jesus on the streets of the capital, adding, 'We're designed to give. God made us that way.' He made me realise how selfish I was. There is nothing more satisfying than blessing other people. Maybe we can offer them a meal, help them with a problem, or pray with them. We should never stop giving. For a Christian, to stop giving is the same as to stop breathing. Spiritually, we die.

Abram certainly became a blessing. Many people were enriched by meeting him. And you and I are living in the good of that today. He is still blessing us every day from beyond the grave.

5. *'I will bless those who bless you, and whoever curses you I will curse'*

One of my children came home from school one day and told me he had been bullied by some other children. 'I'm going straight after them,' I told him. 'Anyone who messes with you messes with me.' This sounded like a threat from a Mafia hitman, but in fact it meant pretty much the same as God's promise to Abram: 'I will bless those who bless you, and whoever curses you I will curse.'

God is very protective towards his children. He dotes on us and will go out of his way to keep us safe. This does not mean that he will not sometimes allow persecution and suffering to develop us into the people he wants us to be. But our concerns, crises, cries and fears are his. If anyone messes with us, they mess with him! If we don't understand this, then we have missed out on an important aspect of his father love. It means that we can tell people who persecute us, 'I'm going to tell my dad about you,' just like we used to say in the playground. And we can have complete confidence that our heavenly Dad is on our case.

We see the same principle operating on an international scale. Every government that has persecuted the Jews has fallen, right to this day. Hitler tried and failed. The Russian government, which had a national policy of persecuting Jews, is now a shambles. During the Six Day War, tiny Israel utterly destroyed the combined efforts of the Arab nations nearby. Although we know that we are God's chosen people now, he still regularly demonstrates that his promises to Abram's descendants hold good. Mess with them and you mess with him!

6. 'All peoples on earth will be blessed through you'

The blessing that came from Abram's life continued to flow long after he died. His seed produced the Messiah and, through Jesus, the whole world is still being blessed. Most of the laws in the Western world are based on Jesus' teachings. Even our calendar is set around him. Nations that identify themselves as Christian generally prosper. And all this is because of God's promise to one man. Jesus said, 'Your father Abraham rejoiced at the thought of seeing my day; and he saw it and was glad' (John 8:56). Abram clearly had a glimpse of things to come, although I don't think he realised the part he would play.

The apostle Paul understood how we as Christians can enjoy Abram's blessings. He told the Galatians, 'Those who have faith are blessed along with Abraham, the man of faith' (3:9). Be encouraged: if you are a believer today, then God wants to bless you, just as he did Abram. It's your birthright.

Do God's promises work for us?

Sometimes we find that God's promises don't always come to pass. If this is your experience, you're in good company. Abram went through it too. Less than half of God's promises came true in his lifetime.

- God promised him the land of Canaan, but it never really belonged to him. In fact when his wife Sarah died he felt he had to buy some land there to bury her. It was not until hundreds of years later that the Jewish people actually possessed Canaan, under Joshua's leadership.
- God promised him a nation, but all he got was two sons and neither of them came without a struggle.
- God promised him a great name, but that greatness only came after he died. His influence was very limited while he was alive.
- God promised to bless all people on the earth through him, but that promise has taken centuries to fulfil and isn't complete yet.

So Abram did not see answers to many of the things God promised him. He had to be patient and enjoy the rest through faith.

We must learn to do the same. We may only see around half of God's promises come true in our lifetime. The rest may come about after we're dead. This might sound disappointing, but to understand it is a step towards real maturity and a deeper relationship with him. It means that we are learning to trust him, even when we have no apparent reason to. For if we learn to wait without becoming discouraged, we become like the real heroes of faith in Hebrews 11. 'None of them received what had been promised,' we are told (vv.39–40). 'God had planned something better.'

Around 200 years before Abram was born, the people of Babel, located in the same region as Ur, decided to build a magnificent city and a tower (or ziggurat) that reached up to heaven. They wanted to make a name for themselves. They wanted to elevate themselves above God. And they thought that if they lived together in a strong, fortified city it would give them security. They could defend themselves from invading armies and avoid being exiled to other parts of the earth. But God threw a spanner in the works by confusing their language, so they could not understand one another. These were people who tried to find security and status through their own efforts. But it got them nowhere.

Abram did things differently. Rather than build a great city, he walked out on one, exchanging his house for a tent. As a result, God didn't just give him a city, but a nation. Rather than make a name for himself, he became a nobody in a foreign country. As a result, God gave him a name that became known throughout the earth.

God's ways certainly aren't ours. He always seems to do things the wrong way round. This is because building friend-ship with us is central to his dealings with us. He is looking for intimacy and depth with people with characters like his own. And he will use every circumstance to try and achieve it. For our part, we will always find that his plans will bear fruit if we co-operate with them. It's easy to take things into our own hands, but if we do we'll soon find that Psalm 127:1 is true: 'Unless the Lord builds the house, its builders labour in vain.' The people of Babel certainly learned that one the hard way. God's blessing never comes from sweat and labour, but through obedience. There are no short cuts. And he never fails.

Playing our part

So why did God's promises to Abram prove to be so reliable? First, because God himself is reliable. But this is only half the picture. Abram also saw God's promises fulfilled because he played his part. Many of God's promises are conditional. He will only do his bit if we do ours. Sadly, most prophecies you hear in churches today leave out this conditional aspect. Then people become confused and disillusioned when the words don't happen. God is only too keen to keep his side of the promise, but he is often restrained because we don't keep ours. This does not mean he breaks his covenant of love with us. He is unable to do that. It is legally binding from his point of view. But his ability to fulfil his promises is sometimes as much down to us as it is to him.

Abram had to do a number of things to ensure that God's words to him were fulfilled. And even though he failed in some areas, God still persevered with him, demonstrating that loyalty is one of the most important qualities in a friendship.

1. He had to separate himself

God has always called his people to separate themselves from the rest of the world. He wants us to be distinct from those around us so that we can demonstrate that friendship with him means a different way of life. That does not mean to say that we become an inward-looking, exclusive huddle – Abram's household seemed to be open to anyone who wanted to join it. But God is looking for a community that is recognisable because of its love and its different standards of behaviour.

Noah's family was the first to separate itself from the ungodly people around, and the principle has remained ever since. Abram followed his example and separated himself from his culture, his friends and his upbringing. Centuries later, one of the reasons God sent his people into exile in Assyria and Babylon was because they refused to separate themselves from the wicked lifestyles of other tribes and nations around them.

The principle was the same in the New Testament. Paul had no hesitation in quoting from 2 Samuel to make the point to the sin-loving Corinthian church: 'Therefore come out from them and be separate, says the Lord. Touch no unclean thing, and I will receive you' (2 Corinthians 6:17).

Separating ourselves from the world is not always fashionable nowadays, probably because the world offers us so many things that we enjoy. But the Scriptures are clear: we need to be different, making sure, though, that part of that difference is loving and accepting people who don't yet know God for themselves. And we must learn from history. We will never see God's promises fulfilled if we compromise, for compromising on truth means compromising on the very friendship itself.

2. He had to switch his focus from an earthly one to a heavenly one

Abram had every reason to remain in Ur. It was a beautiful town from a worldly point of view. But after his encounter with God's glory, his focus was never the same again. God had called him to another country, but that wasn't all. He was more importantly calling him to a heavenly home – a city whose architect and builder was God himself (Hebrews 11:10). Somehow he glimpsed the new heaven and earth, the new Jerusalem described by John in Revelation 21:1–4. It was this vision that kept him going. It helped him to realise that everything on earth was second rate compared to what was to come, and it enabled him to keep a loose hold and a realistic perspective of earthly things, including the life of his own sons. We hear a lot about vision in churches today, but unless our vision is based on heaven and on eternity, we will always end up disappointed. Earthly things are guaranteed to disappoint us. But having God as a friend never will.

3. He had to show obedience, commitment and trust

No one could ever say that Abram had it easy. His life consisted of difficult decisions, of family conflicts, of struggles and pain. He had to put his faith on the line time after time. He faced problems that had absolutely no human answer. And it wasn't a struggle that lasted a year or two. His difficult journey with God lasted decades and didn't even begin until he was quite an old man. All this required real commitment and perseverance. We will find, like Abram did, that the Christian walk isn't always an easy one. But it is certainly the best one.

4. He had to live a righteous life

God was quite clear to Abram: 'Walk before me and be blameless' (Genesis 17:1). A tough order, especially in an area that was beset with sexual immorality and idol worship. It would have been easy for him to compromise and sin like everyone else. He could have easily turned to worship the gods of his father. But apart from the occasional lapses he remained steadfast and was rewarded for it.

If we are struggling with our relationship with God and are not seeing his promises fulfilled in our lives, we should take time to ask him if there is anything that is locking out his blessings. He will always keep his side of a promise if we keep ours.

3

Exploring the Land

Abram rubbed his eyes and wondered if they were playing tricks on him. After all, eye complaints were not uncommon among desert-dwellers, and he had spent a long time in the desert regions before arriving in Canaan. But deep down he knew he wasn't imagining it. The stranger who had stopped by for some food, drink and a chat had disappeared. He had literally vanished into thin air as he waved goodbye and set off on his journey.

This was no ordinary stranger, Abram thought. And suddenly his heart beat faster. He was convinced of it: the stranger had been God himself. He recognised the glory of his Lord that he had sensed for the first time in Ur, all those years ago.

So God himself had visited him, just as a friend would. Abram shook his head in amazement and then laughed. It had been many years since God had given him those great promises back in Ur, and now he had spoken again, just when Abram was wondering if he had imagined it all and had uprooted his family and taken them on a long journey for nothing.

He tried to remember what the stranger had looked like, but the impressions had already started to fade from his mind.

Anyway, it was what the man had said that was more important. 'To your offspring, I will give this land,' he had told him,
quite unexpectedly, as they sat talking about this and that in the
shade of Abram's tent.

Abram gazed at the green fields and forests that surrounded
the great city of Shechem, situated beyond him in the lush
green valley. The mountains Gerizim and Ebal stood like
awesome towers in the distance on either side, sparkling
majestically in the sunshine. Off to the west was the shimmering blueness of the Mediterranean Sea, just over 20 miles
away. It certainly was a beautiful land – far richer and more
abundant than anything he had left behind. Maybe Abram was
starting to learn that if you give things up for God, he will
always give you more back if you are prepared to wait.

It had been several months since Abram and his fellow-
travellers had tentatively entered Canaan. Rather than take the
easy option and settle down, Abram decided to continue his
journey along the King's Highway trade route, which linked
Egypt with Mesopotamia, all the way to the pastoral valley of
Shechem in the region of Gilgal. The fact that he stuck to tradi-
tional routes perhaps reveals an important point to us: that
God's paths are often the most obvious ones.

Abram remembered how he and his household had literally
gasped in amazement at the beauty of the valley when they had
first seen it. It had burst into view as they walked round some
rocks: refreshing streams, gurgling their way down the mountains; acres of lush green fields, spangled with flowers of a
hundred colours; olive groves and orchards, from which the
delicious tangy aroma of lemons and oranges filled the air. And
God was telling him that this land was his! Try telling that to
the war-loving Canaanites! Still, God had spoken to him, right
in the middle of this pagan foreign land, and if God had
spoken, then the rest was up to him. All Abram could do was

believe what he had said and act on it as best he could.

Abram felt he needed to do something to mark this special event. After all, it wasn't every day that the Lord God visited his people. So he called out to some servants who were busy tending some cattle: 'Go to that stream and pick out some stones. Big ones – as big as you can carry. Bring them here.'

His wife Sarai emerged from the tent where she had been doing some weaving. 'What are you doing?' she asked curiously, watching the servants hurrying off to the stream.

'We're building an altar to our God,' said Abram. 'He has just appeared to me. In fact he stood more or less where you're standing now!' Sarai's eyes grew wide with astonishment. 'That man who was here a few minutes ago,' resumed Abram excitedly, 'that was God himself. And he told me that this land, Canaan, is ours!'

'But we can't build an altar just here,' said Sarai. 'This is a place where the Canaanites worship their gods. I've seen their altars in the groves. You can smell their animal sacrifices at night. They even offer human sacrifices.'

Abram thought for a moment. His wife had a point. They were camping in the heavily wooded area of Moreh, near a huge sprawling terebinth tree, almost 10 metres round and 6.5 metres high. The tree was famous throughout the region as a focus of occult activity, and divination was regularly carried out beneath its mighty branches. It certainly was a place where the Canaanites, a hostile race, regularly worshipped their gods.

After considering the matter for a few moments, Abram suddenly stood up straight and declared, 'Let's make it clear to everybody that we worship the one true God, not these worthless idols. We had enough of them in Ur and in Haran. Let's get on with it.'

After an hour, the altar was complete – a huge mound of smooth rocks and stones, glistening in the hot sunshine. The servants who had built it stopped for a rest, sweat still dripping from their foreheads as they drank feverishly out of the water bottles. After they had rested for a while, Abram gathered his clan around him and they worshipped the one true God, right in the middle of hostile enemy territory in one of the Bible's first displays of spiritual warfare.

* * *

That public act was a lesson for all of us. When we engage in prayer and spiritual warfare we tend to go into a room or a church hall and bellow at the devil from behind closed doors. I remember once spending weeks binding and loosing a disturbing occult poster in a shop window. I cursed it, rebuked it, commanded it to go – everything you can think of, in fact – but it stubbornly stayed put. Eventually, when I bothered to listen, God told me to go and speak to the shopkeeper and tell him why the poster was offensive and potentially dangerous. I did, and ended up witnessing to him. He took the poster down straight away. I learned that spiritual warfare is best done on the enemy's turf.

The apostle Paul followed the same principle on his missionary journeys. In virtually every town he visited, he took the devil on right in the middle of enemy territory. In Athens, he went straight to the Areopagus, a key centre of idolatry, and engaged in spiritual warfare by proclaiming the gospel. The result was that a number of people were snatched from the devil's kingdom and into God's (Acts 17:34). Paul found the truth of Moses' words given to us centuries earlier: 'Every place where you set your foot will be yours' (Deuteronomy 11:24). This is why Jesus told us to *go* into the world and tell everybody the good news of having a friendship with him. He never told the world to come to church! We need to act on his instructions and follow Abram's example, and take our worship and our warfare out of our church buildings and onto the streets.

Don't alter the altar!

I once spent an afternoon building a rockery and it nearly killed me, so I am glad God doesn't require us to build altars any more. In the Old Testament, an altar served several purposes. Primarily, it was a landmark. It drew people's attention to the god for whom it had been built. Nowadays our church buildings fulfil a similar role to a degree, although I think that *we* are the best way of revealing God to people. We are like walking altars – or should be. Our lifestyles should make it clear whom we worship, by the way we demonstrate Jesus' love and power.

Altars were also a place of worship. Now, because of Jesus' sacrifice on the cross, we do not have to build piles of rocks, kill animals or see a priest in order to worship God. Romans 12:1 tells us that we worship him by offering ourselves as 'living sacrifices'. You don't even need a worship group or a sound system to do it!

But altars have another role. They are a place of cleansing. After all, how can you worship a holy God if you are full of unholiness? Right through the Old Testament, people cleansed themselves before they worshipped him. In Moses' day, a bronze basin of water was placed near the altar, and the priests had to wash their hands before they went into the Tent of Meeting to worship the Lord. This washing was in addition to offering animal sacrifices. The same principle applies to us today. Although we do not need to offer sacrifices to approach God (Jesus has done this for us already), we do need to wash ourselves first, by cleansing our hearts and minds from the contamination of the world with the water of God's word. Paul describes it well in 2 Corinthians 7:1, '. . . let us purify ourselves from everything that contaminates body and spirit.' There is a cleansing that Jesus does for us, but there is also a cleansing that we must do for ourselves. It is the basis of worship and we need to come to the cross every day (1 Corinthians 15:31b). Then we can approach our God with clean hands and a pure heart (Psalm 24:4).

Another thing we can learn from Abram is that he nailed his colours to the mast very soon after he entered Canaan. It was a risky thing to do. It would have been safer for him to keep quiet and only mention his faith with God on a 'need-to-know' basis. But maybe he realised that this approach could lead to compromise later on. I have always found that if you don't tell people you are a Christian at the outset of a new job or when you move house, you end up never telling them at all.

Abram followed this principle of being up-front with his faith again and again. During those early years in Canaan he repeatedly built altars as he travelled to different parts of the country. It was his way of declaring to people, and the devil, 'This is what I stand for.'

I doubt if Abram realised the significance of his actions when he 'took' Shechem for God by building an altar there. His actions had a territorial significance that lasted for centuries. We need to remember this when we build our churches and plant new ones. As we establish God's presence in an area, we are not just affecting society now. Our actions can affect future generations as well.

Years after Abram camped there, Shechem became a city of enormous national importance. It was situated around 40 miles north of Jerusalem and was strategically located on both the north–south and east–west trade routes. It did not have any natural defences and so relied on high walls and other man-made devices to keep enemies out. It drew its water from a cave in Mount Gerizim and its food from the nearby plain of Askar, and it was because supplies were so plentiful and easy to find that it was occupied for hundreds of years.

During this time, it was a place of great importance to God and his people. Its position, sandwiched between Mount Gerizim and Mount Ebal, formed a natural ampitheatre, which gave Joshua an ideal platform from which to read the Book of the Law to the whole of Israel, as commanded by Moses (Deuteronomy 27:12–13). Mount Gerizim is called the Mount of Blessing, and Mount Ebal is called the Mount of Cursing. Shechem represented a place of choice for God's people – the same choice we still have to make every day.

After Israel entered the Promised Land, Joseph's bones were taken back to Shechem to be buried in a plot of ground that Jacob had purchased (Joshua 24:32). They remain there to this day. Abram's grandson Jacob also dug a well there, and it wasn't just a few feet deep either. It was probably almost 92 metres deep and around 1.5 metres wide, cut into solid rock. It has been filled in with stones over the centuries.

In 928, after King Solomon died, his son Rehoboam went to Shechem to be confirmed as King of Israel, and it later became the capital city for King Jeroboam. The Assyrians captured it in 722 BC, and the mixed marriages that followed produced the Samaritan race, which the Jews despised. To this day, Samaritan priests still celebrate the Passover on Mount Gerizim.

Many years later, Jesus stopped for a drink from Jacob's well. This was long after the city of Shechem had been destroyed, but the site still retained its strategic spiritual importance. He gave his first talk about worship there to the woman at the well (John 4:23–24) and he conducted a two-day evangelistic revival crusade there.

The word 'Shechem' means 'shoulder', a Hebrew symbol of

strength. And Moreh (the site of Abram's first altar) means 'instruction'. The fact that they appear together in Abram's first stopping place in Canaan is significant. We will find the strength to live the pilgrim life that Abram led by receiving instruction from him and other people.

Abram could never have realised the investment he was making in the lives and futures of his descendants when he offered that simple act of worship at Moreh. We too will never understand the impact our simple acts of worship will have on history.

When I read the account of Abram's life I become really jealous of the fact that God actually appeared to him – not just once, but several times. It doesn't seem fair! I can remember as a young Christian spending ages on my knees asking God to appear to me, or at least to speak to me audibly. But he never did. And the chances are he never will – not to me and not to you. Why?

The Bible is like a journey: a continuing account of how God has revealed himself to his people over the centuries. And my view is that he needed to do so more clearly and more tangibly for people like Noah and Abram, who were right at the beginning of this journey of revelation. After all, they had no reference points – no Scriptures and few people, if any, to tell them about God. So he needed to make his presence obvious.

As God's people have continued with that journey, God has continued to reveal himself in different ways: through the Law, the prophets, through miracles and ultimately through Jesus and the Bible. He is continuing to do so now through you his church.

You and I are a long way into that journey of revelation. We have the whole of history to draw on in our search for God. Because of this, we do not need the personal, face-to-face visitations that Abram experienced. We live by faith, and in some ways, perhaps, more than he did.

God's turf . . .

When God gave Canaan to Abram, he certainly gave him a wonderful land. It was lush, fertile, prosperous and strategically placed from a commercial point of view. The Jewish people did not call it a land of milk and honey for nothing. Even today, visitors to Palestine marvel at its beauty.

In Abram's time it was a country made up of many independent city-states, many with their own dialects and usually ruled by kings. These monarchies were powerful. They had elaborate courts and wide powers for military conscription, requisitioning land, collecting taxes and the like. The inhabitants tended to live in family units, either in cities, towns or villages, and came from one of two social classes. They were either upper class or semi-slaves, who worked as herdsmen, butchers, bakers and builders. Idolatry was rife. The main gods and goddesses were Baal, Asherah, Astarte and Anath – gods of either sex or war. This shaped the type of people Canaan produced: violent and immoral.

Canaan became the Promised Land to the Jews. And there are features about it that can help us as God leads us into our promised land.

1. Canaan is a place of conflict

Mention the 'Promised Land' to some people and they assume it will be a place to put their feet up and enjoy God's blessing. I wish this were the case! The Promised Land certainly is a place where God wants to bless us, but it is also somewhere that is full of God's enemies. Abram soon discovered this as he arrived in Canaan. Genesis 12:6 tells us, 'At that time the Canaanites were in the land.' In fact Abram generally lived at peace with the inhabitants of 'his' country. God never told him to wage a military conquest against them. Genesis shows us that he had good relations with the Canaanites, Perizzites, Philistines or Hittites. He was respected as the leader of a large and wealthy household and was treated as an equal by other tribes and kings. He was certainly not a man of war, although he showed that he was willing to have a fight when he needed to. God left it to Joshua to take on the role of warrior and conquer the Promised Land, but he and his armies did not finish the job. When they entered Canaan, God ordered them to exterminate all the tribes. They didn't carry out the order, though, and were hounded and afflicted by them for hundreds of years. These pagan tribes were always a thorn in Israel's side.

We will find, as the Jews did, that our promised land will be full of giants, walled cities and enemy tribes. These things may be issues in our characters or they may be external pressures. Either way, we need to be prepared for a Christian life of perpetual conflict with our flesh, the devil and the world.

2. Canaan is a place of decision

After Abram left Shechem, Genesis 12:8 tells us that he pitched his tent with 'Bethel on the west and Ai on the east'. There is enormous spiritual significance in this. Bethel means 'house of God' and Ai means 'ruin'. As Christians, we are constantly caught between these two places. We can either choose God or choose ruin. It can never be both. And it can change from day to day, from minute to minute. Am I doing what God wants or what I want? Is it his will or mine? The choice has always been there since the Garden of Eden, and always will be.

3. Canaan is a place of change

Our Christian life is one of constant change – or it should be. That does not mean that we should be looking to change jobs, homes, churches and partners every five minutes. God wants us to lead stable lifestyles, to be people who can see things through. But stability should never give us an excuse to get stuck in the rut of tradition and religiosity or to have hearts that are so inflexible we oppose change when it comes. I once heard of a church that split because the leader wanted to change the chairs! Another hit serious problems when the new vicar moved a potted plant from one side of the hall to the other. I believe God hates stubborn resistance like this. We need to remember that we are on a journey of change that will never end until we get to heaven. This is an exhausting thought in some ways, but a very exciting one in others.

I am always completely mystified by churches and Christians who resist change. A Christian resisting change is like a fish resisting water. It is part of our job description and should come naturally to us. It should be something we hunger for. Yet sadly church history is littered with the skeletons of churches and groups that refused to change and were left behind when God moved on.

When Abram got to Canaan he kept going. Had I been him, I'd have settled down the minute I crossed the border. After all, I had done what God had asked, hadn't I? I'd completed the journey! But he continued with his. And he carried on living in a tent because his travels never ended, even though he had the money to buy or build a house and probably would have welcomed a more comfortable place to live in his old age. He was always on the move, and so should we be in our spiritual walk with God.

Enoch walked with God for 300 years (Genesis 5:22), and you can't walk without moving or going somewhere. In the New Testament, Paul told the Galatians (5:25) to keep in step with the Spirit. You can't keep in step if you are not moving. We are not called to mark time! If we are not moving, then we've become settlers, settling for what we've got, and we are not living the lives God wants us to live. Constant change is here to stay!

Abram the prophet

Abram lived an extraordinary life, probably without realising it a lot of the time. So many of his ordinary actions provided glimpses into the future; they were enormously prophetic.

During his early days in Canaan, he visited Shechem, Bethel and the Negev (Genesis 12: 6–9). We don't know why he chose these places or why he went to them in this order. Maybe he didn't either, although he may well have been acting under divine guidance. But in fact he was mapping out the territory that eventually belonged to Israel under Joshua, centuries later. For when Israel went into the Promised Land, we read, 'Then Joshua sent them off, and they went to the place of ambush and lay in wait between Bethel and Ai . . . Then Joshua built on Mount Ebal [at Shechem] an altar to the Lord' (Joshua 8:9, 30). It seems that Abram's journey prophetically forecast the future boundaries for God's people.

Abram acted prophetically in many other ways too. He entered into a covenant of friendship with God, as both Jews and Christians have done ever since. He went to Egypt and met the Pharaoh, as Moses later did. And of course he offered up his only son as a sacrifice, just as God did with Jesus.

We too probably do not realise the spiritual significance of many of the ordinary things we do every day. But if we are walking with God as Abram was, our actions may have repercussions years later, in ways we could never have imagined.

4

Failure and Compromise

The little boy looked into his father's eyes with growing terror. Surely his daddy wouldn't kill him. But there was something about his father's expression that he had never seen before. Gaunt. Desperate. Driven.

The father tightened his grip around his struggling son's neck, reached inside his robes and pulled out a long-bladed knife. Quickly, clinically he slit his son's throat. Blood spurted everywhere and the boy, aged only five, collapsed to the ground, retching and screaming. Within seconds, he was dead. Later that evening his weeping mother roasted parts of his body to feed her starving family.

Famine had struck Canaan.

Some miles away in the Negev region, not far from Beersheba, Abram and his family sat silently round their campfire, looking distastefully at the meal their servants had given them in stone bowls. A few scraps of disgusting looking meat, with dove's dung to serve as vegetables, washed down with a few drops of scarce water gathered from that morning's dew. The drought had been going on for months and Abram could not remember the last time it had rained. The wells had all run dry. Famines were not uncommon in this part of the world. There was no irrigation system, so people had to rely on the rain storms for their water supplies, along with the heavy seasonal mists that rolled in from the Mediterranean Sea.

'What meat is this?' Abram asked a servant girl.

'Donkey's head, my lord,' she replied. Abram spat in disgust. No one ever ate donkeys' heads. Even poor people avoided them if they could. But these were desperate times. Abram's household had suffered months of drought in the normally fertile plains of the Negev. Crops had withered to dust and Abram's massive stock of cows, sheep and donkeys had dwindled as the animals starved to death one by one. Abram looked at the piles of animal bones a few hundred yards away, shook his head again and began eating the revolting concoction that had been set before him. The choice was simple: eat it or die of starvation, just as hundreds of other people in the region had done already.

Abram rose to his feet. His mind began to wander back to his comfortable life in Ur, but he rejected that tempting train of thought immediately. No, that was in the past. It was time to act. He would go to Egypt, a short distance away, even though it was a trip that was not often made by Canaanites. He had heard it was a place where there was always plenty of food because of its sophisticated irrigation system and fertile land regularly watered by the Nile floods.

Trust God? It didn't even enter his thinking.

* * *

You sometimes hear people say that when you become a Christian you receive an instant scratch card to an inheritance of never-ending victory, blessing, prosperity and success. 'Give your life to Jesus,' I once heard an evangelist say, 'and all your problems will go away.' If only this were true! My experience was that when I became a Christian my problems were just beginning, and God was the cause of most of them, although he did help me to solve them as he got to work on different aspects of my character. Those who say differently are usually just better at pretending than the rest of us. For most of us, the Christian life is one where we find joy, peace and victory in the middle of pain, pressure and difficulty – not instead of them. And yet it's easy to feel condemned or short-changed by God when our inheritance is not all we hoped it would be.

Abram faced the same problem. He obeyed God and went to Canaan to receive his inheritance. And what did he experience there? Victory and blessing? Far from it! Famine and a barren wife – not exactly signs of God's blessing. Quite the reverse in fact, for in the Old Testament both of these afflictions were seen as signs of God's disapproval. Had Abram wanted prosperity and comfort, he would have done better to stay in Ur, or Haran perhaps. And maybe he wondered, as we do, if his problems were a sign that he had gone out of God's will. Perhaps he was tempted at times to turn his camel round and go back home. But he kept his nerve, stayed the course and learned that even when you get to the place of your inheritance, you still have to keep on trusting God for food to eat every day.

Obeying God's word is not always the easy option. Obedience often leads to obstacles, hardships and problems, and disobedience can often appear to be easier. Jonah took the soft option when God told him to go to Nineveh. Rather than face possible persecution and death in that wicked city, he caught a boat and headed off in the opposite direction, and even managed to sleep peacefully during a life-threatening storm (Jonah 1:5). Feeling 'peace' is not always a sign that you are in God's will!

If you look at the lives of people in Scripture, you usually find that following God was costly and fraught with difficulty. God did not always give them quick-fix solutions or 'name it and claim it' victories. When baby Jesus' life was under threat from King Herod (Matthew 2:13), God told Joseph to escape to the safety of Egypt. That meant that he and Mary had to abandon their home in Nazareth and live in a foreign land for a number of years until King Herod died. The easier solution would have been for God to bring his 'victory' into the situation by removing Herod immediately. This would have meant an easier ride for baby Jesus and would have spared the lives of many Hebrew babies. But God had other plans. He always does. And they are not always the most obvious or the most 'victorious'.

* * *

Abram gasped in amazement. He had not seen anything like this before. Ur had been a magnificent city, but it didn't compare with this. He looked round at the ornate buildings, playing fountains and dominant statues, and thought that Thebes, situated in the Delta region of the River Nile, must be the finest city on earth.

He and his travellers huddled under an archway and gazed around in awe. The streets were a hubbub of noise and activity. Carts laden with grain jostled with one another along the roadways. Slaves engaged in vast building projects screamed as the muscular slave-drivers lashed them mercilessly. Traders shouted their wares in the colourful cacophony of a nearby market. The crowds glanced up momentarily as a contingent of soldiers in chariots clattered round the corner, but the bustle resumed as they went off into the distance towards a heavily fortified garrison.

So this was Egypt! Abram had often heard about its grandeur from merchants who visited Haran, but he never expected it to be like this. And there was no shortage of food here. Far from it.

Cautiously he ushered his household through the streets towards the market, where stalls laden with leeks, garlic, bread, meat and all kinds of fruit beckoned invitingly. Abram's mouth began to water and he felt pangs of hunger. He had learned to live with stomach pains for weeks now. But not any more. It was time to eat! He went up to a swarthy stallholder and began the inevitable process of bartering for some food. Later his family sat down in a quiet square and enjoyed their first proper meal for a long time.

Abram wondered how long they should remain in Egypt. There was certainly no need to hurry back to Canaan and it held little appeal anyway, with famine still gripping the land. And he certainly did not relish the prospect of the uphill trek through the Nile delta and mountainous regions. But deep inside he felt twinges of fear and unease. God hadn't actually told him to go to Egypt. Maybe he should have stayed in Canaan and trusted God for his food and water. It hadn't been an easy decision. But anyway, he thought, as he ate a succulent pomegranate, he was here now and there was nothing he could do about it. And his household needed to eat.

But he knew he had compromised again, just as he had done when he allowed his father and Lot to accompany him on his journey. He looked thoughtfully at Sarai, who was laughing with a slave girl as they ate their food. Once again he sensed that nagging fear. She was so beautiful, even in her advancing years, and he had no doubt that the lustful Egyptians would find her fair complexion irresistible compared with the copper-skinned women of their own race. What if the Egyptians saw her and took her into the royal harem? He had heard of it happening before. Tradition in this part of the world allowed men to kill other men and take their wives as their own. Abram shuddered again at the prospect and was glad that he had hatched a contingency plan with

Sarai several days earlier, before they had entered Egypt.

'I know what a beautiful woman you are,' he had told her. 'When the Egyptians see you, they will say, "This is his wife." Then they will kill me but will let you live. Say you are my sister, so that I will be treated well for your sake and my life will be spared because of you.'

Abram smiled wryly to himself as he recalled the scheme. Well, it was true, wasn't it? Sarai was his sister – or his half-sister, at least. And the fact that she did not have any children made it even easier for him to pass her off as being unmarried. So everything would be all right. He would be safe. Local customs also dictated that a man could only take a single woman if he negotiated with her family first. So the Egyptians could not touch Sarai without his permission, and this would give him time to escape if necessary.

But what Abram didn't realise was that in hatching a plan to deceive the Egyptians, what he was really doing was deceiving himself. And God.

* * *

I remember telling a friend of mine about my dreams of having a 'healing ministry'. After hearing me explain how I would raise the dead and see the blind healed, he interrupted with a sobering dose of reality. 'How come you've still got a cold, then?' he asked. And he had a point. I thought I had faith for the 'big' things, but could not even make God's promises work in my own life. It's so easy to get into this way of thinking. We become so full of vision for the great things that we miss the opportunity to grow in the everyday issues of life – things like seeing God heal our families when they are sick or paying the bills on time.

Abram suffered from the same problem. When it came to big challenges, like uprooting and moving from Ur and believing God's promises to make him into a great nation, he rarely wavered. But when it came to the practical things, like feeding his family and trusting God to protect his wife, he failed miserably and compromised. When famine struck Canaan, Abram did not seek God, but rushed ahead, acted independently and went to Egypt. He probably thought he was acting wisely, but in fact he was putting his own life and Sarai's in great danger. And rather than trust God to keep them safe, he resorted to deceit and lies and turned his back on their friendship.

He also failed to depend on the promises God had made him earlier. After all, God had guaranteed to keep him safe when he told him, 'I will bless those who bless you, and whoever curses you I will curse.' Abram found, as we do, that hearing God's promises is one thing, but believing them when the going gets tough is another. It's sometimes easier to look at circumstances rather than at God and to take matters into our own hands – a tendency that Abram frequently displayed and one that he sowed into his son Isaac, who also lied to save his skin in similar circumstances years later (Genesis 26:7). Parents need to realise that their children will normally end up doing the things they do, such is the power of the hereditary line.

* * *

Pharaoh Acthoes awoke with a start. He had dozed off after consuming a sumptuous dinner and several glasses of wine. But now a servant was nervously calling his attention.

'What is it? Why have you woken me up?'

The servant's colour ran from his cheeks. He knew that Pharaoh had the right to have him executed if he wanted to. But he also knew that the King often rewarded those who made him happy. And, the servant thought, this news would make him very happy.

He began speaking, nervously: 'Word has come to me, my lord, and some of your princes have heard it too. I thought I should come and tell you before they do . . .'

'Tell me what?' Pharaoh showed signs of getting angry.

'About a beautiful woman, my lord.' Pharaoh sat up immediately and listened carefully.

'She is not from here, my lord. She comes all the way from Chaldea and is not like the Egyptian women. Although she wears a veil, I hear that she is fair skinned and of outstanding beauty. I thought you might desire her, my lord.'

Pharaoh did not hesitate. His appetite for women was well known and he was getting bored with Egyptians. He was not going to miss this opportunity. 'A veil?' he said with surprise. Egyptian women of that era did not wear veils to cover their faces. 'How unusual! Well, we must discover what mysteries lie beneath it! Bring her to me. Quickly.' The servant went away smiling. Perhaps promotion might be his reward.

Within an hour a rider on horseback had been dispatched to find Sarai and bring her into the royal courts, proving to Abram the truth of the words written in the book of Job: 'What I feared has come upon me; what I dreaded has happened to me.' You often find that the things you fear most in life, like poverty, cancer, redundancy and accidents, are the very things that occur. That's because fear can yield the same fruit as faith, and you get what you expect.

Later on, Abram and Sarai walked nervously into Pharaoh's throne room. The decadent grandeur took their breath away. Ornate columns, each inlaid with solid gold and glazed with green, blue and red, towered above them. Ominous statues of gods and animals made of different coloured stones stood against the brightly painted walls. Beneath their feet, spectacular coloured pictures of plants and birds adorned the floor.

They approached Pharaoh's throne and bowed and kissed

the floor beneath his feet in the customary way that a courtier had explained to them when they had arrived at the palace. Pharaoh's eyes rested upon Sarai and utterly devoured her. She avoided his gaze, her heart pounding. How on earth could her husband put her in this position, she wondered?

Reluctantly Pharaoh turned his eyes from her and addressed Abram, politely and with considerable respect. 'Who are you?' he enquired.

Abram told the great ruler their names and where they were from, and then explained how Sarai was his sister. He felt his mouth grow dry as the words left him, and a sense of regret overwhelmed him.

'I would like to take your sister into my courts as my wife,' said Pharaoh. 'Under my country's laws I have the right to take any woman I like, without permission.' Abram's heart sank. His plan was already going wrong. 'However,' resumed Pharaoh, beckoning a slave to come and fan him with a beautifully decorated fan made of peacock feathers, 'I have regard for the fact that you are from another land and you are not subject to our customs. I will therefore honour you by purchasing your sister from you. I will give you as many sheep, oxen, donkeys and camels as you wish, and my best men and women servants. I think you will agree that this is a fair offer.' Pharaoh paused and a smile touched his lips. 'After all, you are about to become my brother-in-law! You are almost part of my family! Do you accept this offer?'

Abram nodded. What else could he do? If he said no, he had no doubt that Pharaoh would take Sarai anyway. Two servants came and escorted Abram from the throne room. Tears welled up in his eyes as he turned and nodded farewell to Sarai. He caught her eye momentarily. Her expression was a mixture of fear and contempt. He carried on walking.

Outside, the sun was setting across Egypt and Abram sat

alone in the landscaped palace gardens, unable to cope with his thoughts. The enormity of his foolishness suddenly overwhelmed him. Not only had he turned his back on one of God's promises by disobeying him and walking out of Canaan, the land God had given him, but now he had sold his wife, and in doing so was despising another of God's precious promises made all those years ago. The words 'I will make you a great nation' came back to his mind. To start a nation he needed an heir. To produce an heir he needed a wife, and he had just sold her! He turned his eyes to the sky. 'Oh my God,' he whispered. 'What have I done?' He knew that he had led his wife into a terrible situation and could not get her out, just as his nephew Lot would with his wife years later.

Tears ran down his face as he reflected on his repeated disobedience to God's words. First God had told him to leave his father's household, but he hadn't – he had taken his father and the troublesome Lot with him. Then God had told him to go to Canaan, but he had ended up in Egypt. And now he had lost his only chance to produce a son to continue his line. What kind of friend did that make him?

As the sun sank like an orange fireball on the distant horizon, Abram wiped away his tears and knew he had failed.

What he didn't know was that he was, in fact, learning one of his first major lessons as a pioneer for God: God uses failures.

* * *

Later Abram was to discover that his disobedience, compromise and insistence on doing things his own way did not affect God's covenant promises for his life at all. God could have rejected him, and with good reason, but their friendship went deeper than that. God didn't tell him that he had missed his chance and blown it for ever. He didn't sack him and appoint someone else. Instead he loved him, restored him, and fulfilled his promises anyway. Nothing changed, because our God is the God of the second chance and he keeps his side of his covenant even when we break ours.

It's called grace.

Our success-driven society doesn't understand this concept at all. Achieve your targets, or you're out. Fail and you miss the bonus or the promotion. That's what the world tells us these days.

Sadly, the same thinking is creeping into some churches, including, surprisingly, many churches that were founded on grace teaching. I heard of a situation recently where a leader's church was shut down because he did not meet his growth targets for the year. Another man had his ministerial credentials removed for good after committing adultery. Now adultery is serious and the man certainly needed correction, discipline and a good long time out of leadership to sort out his marriage and his walk with God. But removing his credentials for good ignored the concept of redemption and the second chance. I have no doubt that God will redeem this brother anyway, if he genuinely repents and changes his ways, for God does not treat us as harshly as this church did when we mess up. If he did, Abram, Moses, David and many other good men would not have been good enough for God to use.

With our God there is always a hope and a future, even when we've done wrong. It's called loyalty – another aspect of true friendship.

* * *

It was later that same evening, and Pharaoh had treated his wife-to-be to a sumptuous meal, fine wines and an extravaganza of entertainment. Now they were alone in his bedroom. Again, Sarai avoided his eyes as he moved closer to her and began to kiss her cheeks. He paused, wondering why he suddenly felt feverish.

Suddenly there was a knock on the door.

'Curses!' he shouted.

A servant stood at the door, trembling.

'How dare you interrupt me! You will die for this. You have disobeyed my orders,' Pharaoh seethed.

'But, my lord,' gasped the servant urgently, 'you must come! Quickly! A great sickness has befallen the palace. The princes, your wives, the servants – they are all ill. Some of them are unconscious. The gods must have cursed us!'

Pharaoh suddenly felt weak and began to shiver uncontrollably. He looked at Sarai thoughtfully.

'Send for my diviners,' he whispered to the servant. 'I need to know what, or who, is behind this!' As the servant scurried away, Pharaoh looked again at Sarai. And yet again she avoided his gaze but said a silent prayer of thanks to God as Pharaoh collapsed onto his bed, seriously ill.

The following day Abram was back in the throne room after being summoned urgently by a messenger. As he stood before Pharaoh, he felt a great sense of peace.

Pharaoh came straight to the point: 'What have you done to me? Why didn't you tell me she was your wife? Why did you say "She is my sister," so that I took her to be my wife? Now then, here is your wife.' He pushed Sarai towards him. 'Take her and go!'

The same afternoon Abram and his household left Egypt surrounded by a contingent of Pharaoh's soldiers, which escorted them all the way to the border with Canaan. Abram looked around at the hundreds of animals being herded along by shepherds and at his servants struggling to carry the heavy boxes and silver and gold that Pharaoh had pressed on them before they went. He shook his head in wonder.

Back in the royal courts, Pharaoh did the same, not imagining that the people of Egypt would give riches to God's people in similar fashion several hundred years later. All he knew was that he was dealing with a man who was different from any he had met before – a man who seemed to be under some special kind of favour from his God. His diviners had been quite clear: 'Have nothing to do with him. He could be a threat to your kingdom. Get rid of him, but treat him well or there could be more trouble ahead. After all, if this man's God can inflict curses just for trying to take his wife, what else might he do?' Pharaoh had not wasted a moment in getting Abram and Sarai out of the country with as much wealth as he could find.

As Abram's clan reached the Negev, Abram realised that he was back in God's will again, and that God had kept his word, despite his own disobedience. He had protected him and had blessed him with many times more livestock than he had lost in the famine, plus enormous riches of gold and silver too. Abram smiled. What an amazing God he had. He was giving him another chance.

* * *

Sadly it was the smile of a man who had not learned his lesson. God had shown him grace and kindness, but that outpouring of mercy did not change Abram's heart. Years later, he again resorted to the same deceit of introducing Sarai as his sister to the people of Gerar, and to another king, this time Abimelech. The King of Gerar believed him, just as Pharaoh did, and this time God had to intervene by giving a dream to Abimelech in order to save Sarai.

Abram did what we all do: he took advantage of God's friendship and grace and thought he had got away with it. He saw God's blessings as a sign of approval and didn't change.

What he did not know was that with God there is always a day of reckoning; only next time God would have to deal with him much more severely in order to finally get to his heart.

The encouraging thing, however, is that Abram's sin and failings did not affect God's promises to him at all. God's mercy was so great that even though Abram went off track, God continued looking after him and Sarai, working through their circumstances to bring them back to his original purposes.

It's also wonderful to realise that there is no record whatsoever in the New Testament of Abram's failings. He is only represented as an example of a man of faith and righteousness for us to follow, not as someone who lied and deceived people when the going got tough.

When God promises that he will not remember our sins, he means what he says. He did not keep a record of Abram's and will not keep a record of yours. And if you, like Abram, have gone off track and have compromised on God's word, don't worry. You will eventually find that he will work his purposes out to get you back to where you should be, if you are prepared to play your part. And hopefully you will find that you have learned much along the way.

5

A Friendship Is Restored

'Look, it's still there!' Abram could not conceal his delight.

His vast party of travellers, more than 1,000 men, women and children, had finally made it to the place between Bethel and Ai where he had built his second altar some time ago. And as they stopped for a while on the rocky slopes of the hill, they could see the big pile of rocks in the distance amid the olive groves.

As the servants began unloading baggage from the backs of donkeys, erecting the tents and building simple fences to act as enclosures for their flocks, Abram walked up slowly to the altar and knelt down.

He remained there a long time, deep in thought. He cast his mind back to the last time he had offered sacrifices there. He had been so close to God then, full of faith and hope as he continued his exploration of Canaan. He realised how much ground he had lost in that friendship during his terrible sojourn in Egypt. Sin and mistrust had clouded his relationship with God in Egypt and still he bore the burden of guilt.

He called to one of his servants to bring him a young lamb and, holding it by its neck, he slit its throat. When it was dead he laid it on top of the twigs and branches on the altar and set light to them. And as he knelt in front of the pile of rocks, with dry wood crackling on the fire and smoke billowing around him, he gradually felt his burden of guilt lift from him.

Deep inside he knew that he was back in fellowship with God again. The friendship was restored. He prayed, saying sorry to God for his foolishness and thanking him for delivering him from that dangerous situation in Egypt.

Several months later, a few miles away, two herdsmen squared up to one another in the scorching heat, their eyes blazing as fiercely as the noonday sun.

'My herds were grazing on this land first,' shouted one, waving his staff in anger. Other men began to gather round them, sensing trouble and ready to join in if necessary. 'My master Lot told us to bring the animals here two days ago. It's the only place where there is any pasture for miles!'

'That's why *we* need it,' exclaimed the other man, becoming increasingly agitated. 'Abram was quite clear that we should bring the herds here. It's bad enough with the Canaanites and Perizzites camping in the region, without you coming and taking all the water and the best grass! And remember . . .' the man paused a moment, ready to place his trump card, '. . . remember who is the head of the clan. It's Abram, not your master Lot. We are his servants and we should have first choice.'

There was murmured assent from some of the other herdsmen standing nearby, and the two factions glared at each other angrily. It was a tense moment that could have exploded into violence.

Later that evening, the two herdsmen did what custom dictated and brought their dispute to Abram to judge. He listened carefully to each side and then sighed and stroked his beard wearily. He had been expecting a situation like this. Pharaoh had done him a big favour by giving him vast numbers

of animals, and as a result he had become one of the wealthiest
men in the region – the Bible's first wealthy follower of God.
But feeding them all was another matter, especially in a region
where provisions were scarce. Fights, even wars, over water
and pastures were not uncommon in this part of the world. It
wasn't the herdsmen's fault, he mused. They were only trying
to do their jobs in difficult circumstances. It was not worth
fighting about. He paused and considered what to do.

After a while he said to Lot, 'Let's not have any quarrelling
between you and me, or between your herdsmen and mine, for
we are brothers. Is not the whole land before you? Let's part
company. If you go to the left, I'll go to the right; if you go to
the right, I'll go to the left.' Lot's eyes lit up with delight.
Abram was generously giving him an offer he could not refuse.
From their vantage point at the top of a hill, he looked around
him at the countryside. The land to the east looked good, he
thought, as he gazed at the River Jordan winding its way into
the distance. The river's plains contained field upon field of
different kinds of crops, all with irrigation systems. This had to
be the place, Lot thought. And he had heard that the towns of
Sodom and Gomorrah were exciting places to live.

Finally he decided. 'I'll go to the east and live on the Jordan
plains,' he told his uncle. It was the obvious choice, humanly
speaking. Abram nodded magnanimously. He did not need to
give Lot first choice and there was no doubt that the younger
man had secured the better deal, but Abram felt that his offer
was the best way to achieve peace between the two house-
holds. He was starting to take on God's values and ways of
doing things. God's way was to put others first and try to live in
peace with them. He was discovering that, as with any friendship, if you spend time with someone, you end up becoming
like them. And his faith in God was growing all the time.

Privately, though, he wondered whether Lot would be able

to cope with living so near Sodom and Gomorrah. His nephew still seemed to have an appetite for the lifestyle he had left behind in Ur long ago, despite years away from the place. His faith in God might not be strong enough to cope with the temptations, especially as he was so wealthy. Still, Lot was old enough to make his own decisions. He had to let him go and fend for himself.

The next morning, the two men embraced one another fondly and Abram watched as Lot's household and herds moved slowly off into the distance to start their new life – a life that should have been wonderful, but ended up with his children going away from God, capture by a foreign king, the death of his wife and little evidence of God's blessing. The choices he made might have appeared sensible from a human point of view, but they were certainly not right. 'I wonder if I will ever see him again,' thought Abram. 'If I do, it will only be by chance.'

Later on, Abram set off with his own clan towards the forests of Mamre in Hebron, and when he arrived he followed his usual custom and built an altar, establishing the site as a place for God. Hebron means 'fellowship' – Abram's reward, perhaps, for doing God's will.

Neither he nor Lot could ever have imagined the strange circumstances of their next encounter.

* * *

An angler friend of mine once told me that smarter fish sometimes manage to swim up to the bait dangling temptingly on the end of his hook and have a little taste, before swimming away unharmed. It can be the same with our attitude to sin. When faced with temptation, we resist it and are not hooked by it, but we do allow ourselves a little nibble. Later on we kid ourselves that we did not actually take the bait, which is absolutely true of course, but our actions show us, and God, exactly where our hearts are: we are prepared to flirt with sin a little if we can get away with it.

This was Lot's problem. There was sin in his heart and because he did not deal with it, it eventually dealt with him in the most terrible way. Sin is like that. God warned Cain that it would devour him if he did not master it (Genesis 4:7). I have no doubt that Lot knew exactly what was going on in Sodom and was tempted by it. So he decided to head that way and pitch his tents nearby – just to have a look, of course; not to live there. His actions were a bit like a 'reformed' alcoholic calling in at the pub to remind himself what it looks like – and to witness to his unsaved friends, of course. Perhaps Lot genuinely thought he could handle Sodom and its evil attractions. But it is more likely that he simply had a divided heart, as many of us have: he wanted God and his blessings, but he wanted the world and its sin as well.

Lot loved personal gain more than righteousness. Had he loved righteousness as he should have done, he would have been determined to avoid Sodom and its wicked people at all costs rather than go and camp near it, and have his tent doors looking straight towards them. As a result, he ended up moving into the city. Sin is like that – it gets you there in stages. Like many people, Lot later discovered that material wealth triggered a moral decline. He began with money and ended up getting drunk and committing incest with his daughters. That's why God warns us in 2 Timothy 6:10 that the love of money is the root of all kinds of evil. He does not have a problem with believers being wealthy, but if their hearts are wrong, problems soon follow.

His choice also shows that he was not walking closely enough with God to see things the way God saw them. In 1 Samuel 16:7 it says, 'The Lord does not look at the things man looks at.' In this situation, Lot saw a fertile valley and a city with a great night life. But God saw that people in Sodom were sinning so excessively that they deserved judgement. Later on, when Lot deliberately and blindly moved into the city with his family, he was only able to see that it was a great place to live. Maybe he thought he was *in* the world but not *of* it. But Abram, who was in tune with God, saw impending doom and the need for urgent intercession.

We live in a society that is just as wicked as Sodom was, if not worse. And the world exposes what's in our hearts, for if there is anything inside us that can be seduced by worldly attractions, then we will always remain vulnerable to temptation, and will probably end up first flirting with it, and then giving in.

Of course, we are all good at coming up with all kinds of 'spiritual' reasons as to why it's all right to indulge in worldly pleasures. 'After all, Jesus enjoyed a drink and mixed with prostitutes,' people say. But in fact all we are doing is behaving like the fish that just can't wait to have a little nibble of the bait, and of course a little nibble eventually becomes a big one, because our flesh always craves more of what it should not have.

We all need to make sure we deal honestly with the desires of our hearts and avoid temptation at all costs. This is why Jesus told us to pray that God would not lead us into temptation. If we decide to pitch our tents anywhere near things that tempt us, then sin is virtually guaranteed. We also need to take care not to expose our families and friends to situations they cannot cope with, or lead them into situations they cannot get out of.

Hebrews 1:9 says that God loves righteousness and hates wickedness. We must learn to do the same, otherwise we will always remain vulnerable in this seductive society. Moses went right to the point in Leviticus 10:10 when he said, 'You must distinguish between the holy and the common, between the unclean and the clean.' Sometimes it's hard to tell. And even harder to avoid the things that are evil.

A time to fight ... ?

So Abram and Lot separated. You often hear of Christians going their separate ways in different situations, and this is usually seen as a bad thing. Often it is, for church splits and severed relationships always break God's heart – they are the equivalent of divorce in his eyes. It is terribly sad that disputes among God's people so often result in division and a new church or group emerging. I believe that God would rather not have the new church if strife is the price that has to be paid for it, for what is sown in strife always produces more strife later on. What makes it more unfortunate is that many splits littering our church landscape these days could have been avoided.

Abram and Lot were at loggerheads in the situation described above. They faced a serious and potentially life-threatening situation. They could have gone to war over who should have the best pastures (I know some churches that would have done!). But Abram, using godly wisdom, defused the situation, and in doing so gave us some important pointers on how to solve disputes without bitter conflict. They are radical, but they work:

1. Be willing to back down

Abram had every legal and moral right to have first choice of the land as he was head of the tribe and had total authority over Lot. And yet he set aside his rights. Had he not done so, the situation would have become worse. Someone had to back down, and he decided it would be him. He could have insisted that Lot give way, but he did not. He refused to use his God-given authority in a heavy-handed way, even though he had the right to. Maybe, like me, you can think of countless situations where you have acted differently from this.

2. See peace as more important than anything else

There is no doubt that Abram was in the right in this situation. Had Lot acted correctly, he would have told his herdsmen to keep quiet and submit to Abram's authority as head of their clan. But Abram still chose to submit to his younger, foolhardy nephew and let God sort things out in his own way. I think I would have said, 'Well, I'm in the right, so God must be on my side.' And I know some Christians, churches, streams and even denominations that have taken the same stance in times of conflict. But what I, and they, have failed to appreciate is that peace and unity are always more important to God than who is right and who is wrong. If we are prepared to give way, even to people who are in the wrong, then we can be completely confident that God will have the final say in the end.

3. Love your 'enemies'

Abram genuinely loved Lot, even though I am sure he had serious misgivings about him. This love was one of the reasons he was able to submit to him. It's usually easy to back down where someone you love is concerned. He loved his nephew like the son he had never had, and was probably delighted to treat him as his heir and hand over the best pastures to him. The heart of a father is always to bless his children. And later on Abram showed the full extent of his love for Lot by being prepared to put his own life on the line and rescue Lot when he was taken captive by some foreign kings.

Ask yourself this regarding those people who split your church and went off with all the best people to greener pastures: Do I love them so much that I would risk my life to help them if they were in trouble? If your answer to that question is no, then you are in the wrong, no matter what the dispute was about or who was in the right. For God tells us to love our enemies, to submit to other people and to put others first, and there are no 'small print' get-out clauses in these commands! Remember, Jesus was prepared to back down and be executed, even when he was completely in the right and his enemies were utterly wrong. He was confident enough in his Father's love to leave him to weigh the situation and act justly to resolve it. Who are we to behave any differently?

If you are involved in any kind of dispute at the moment, whether it's in church, family or at work or college, you should not make any decision until you have learned to love the other party – and really love them. This could take months, even years, to achieve. It could end up with them gaining the upper hand, as Lot did. But so what? If you love them, and maybe only God can help you to do it, then there can only be one outcome: peace. God will bless you for it and have the last word in the situation.

4. Have a big heart

Despite his failings Abram was big-hearted enough to let Lot go his own way. We might have persuaded him to stay 'for the kingdom's sake' and convinced him there would be greater strength in numbers. We might have been threatened by Lot's ambitions and feared that he might end up more successful than we are. But Abram was prepared to release his nephew, just as the father was reluctantly prepared to release his child in the story of the Prodigal Son. In fact this conversation between Abram and Lot bears some incredible resemblances to the parable Jesus told hundreds of years later. Maybe Jesus had it in mind when he told it. Sadly, though, Lot never showed a repentant heart like the Prodigal Son did.

With God's upside-down way of doing things, the more tightly we hold on to things, the more likely we are to lose them, whether they are our churches, our children, our leaders or those who want to go and do something different. We may try to hold on to them for all the right reasons (It's God's will; we know best; they might get hurt), but if we are prepared to let them go, in love and peace and more importantly with our ongoing blessing, then God will reward us. In fact he will give back to us more than we ever gave away, for that's his written guarantee (Luke 6:38).

Many churches and groups have gone to war over the last 30 years because leaders were not prepared to let people go unconditionally and with their blessing. Promising moves of God have either been slowed down or destroyed in the cross-fire and aftermath. Jesus was once faced with a similar situation, recorded for us in Luke 9:49ff. The disciple John reported to Jesus that he had seen a man casting out demons in Jesus' name. 'We tried to stop him, because he is not one of us,' John proudly told his Master. He was probably expecting a pat on the back for sticking to the rules and keeping deliverance within their special group. But Jesus was big-hearted enough to say, 'Do not stop him, for whoever is not against you is for you.'

He had a big heart – a heart that was prepared to release, just as Abram did before them. And because of that they missed out on nothing. God always makes up the difference, and adds some more on top. His attitude was: so long as the job gets done, who cares who does it or which group they are in? Ours should be the same. We should declare war on that tendency in our hearts to draw a circle round our group, church or stream and tie everything up with stifling structure to contain everything inside it.

Groups and churches that have divided in the past should remember that if their separation was not carried out with love, peace and unity, then *both* parties are in the wrong and will both need to repent before they can see God's fullest blessing on their lives and their work again. For it's only when there is true unity of heart that God commands a blessing (Psalm 133:1).

5. Be secure in God's promises

One of the reasons Abram was able to allow Lot to go was because he knew God would underwrite his decisions. He could be sure of this because he had seen him do it in Egypt.

God had promised Abram that he would be blessed. He had promised he would make him into a great nation. He had told him that Canaan was his. And Abram was no doubt certain that these promises would hold good, whether Lot stayed or went, or which part of the land he chose. He was completely secure in the fact that nothing Lot did or did not do could possibly affect the outcome of God's plans. So why fight Lot? What would be the point?

We should learn from Abram that if we are prepared to trust God and back down even when we are in the right, then it is impossible to end up the loser, because God will always keep his word and fulfil his promises if we keep our hearts right.

* * *

It was a hot afternoon and Abram was doing what all shepherds did – he was sleeping in the shade of his tent doorway as Sarai and some of the women servants were busy preparing the evening meal. They were staying in a wooded area of Hebron, on land occupied by a Canaanite chief called Mamre who had formed an alliance with Abram's tribe.

Suddenly a servant ran up to their tent and shook Abram

gently. 'My lord, wake up! Wake up!' There was urgency in his voice.

Abram woke up and rubbed his eyes. 'What is it?' he asked kindly. He knew his servant would not wake him unless there was a good reason.

'It's Lot, my lord!'

Abram sat up with a start. Was there news of his nephew? 'What about him?' he replied. The last he had heard of Lot was that he was living in Sodom with his family. He had not seen him for years.

'He's been captured by a coalition of kings led by Kedorlaomer. They have ransacked Sodom and Gomorrah and taken dozens of prisoners, including Lot. One of the men escaped and came to you for help. He is over there having something to eat.' The servant gestured towards a tent on the other side of their encampment.

'Kedorlaomer, eh?' Abram nodded in recognition. He had heard about this war-mongering king and his allies before. They had been causing trouble in the region for years, but so far had left Abram and his vast clan alone. 'Well, we'll have to go and get him, won't we?'

Yet again Abram displayed his love and commitment to Lot. Even though his nephew had gone his own way and had now obviously been taught a lesson, Abram was still there to help him when he certainly did not deserve it.

The servant's face drained of colour as he realised the implications of his master's decision. No one fought Kedorlaomer and his allies and won.

Abram's clan suddenly became a hive of activity. He moved quickly around the tents, marshalling his fighting men. They had been born in his tribe and were totally loyal to him – they would die for him if necessary. An hour later he had marshalled 318 of them from the thousand or so people who lived with him. Abram and his servants began handing out weapons, ready for the battle ahead. There was an air of nervous anticipation as he issued the young men their orders.

'Our information is that Kedorlaomer and his men are camped near Dan, on the northern borders of Canaan, around 120 miles away. It will take us about five days to travel there. When we get there we will divide into two groups and attack them at night, coming in from two directions at once. They should be asleep, so we will have surprise on our side and should cause maximum panic and confusion. As soon as you get into their camp, cut the ropes of their tents so they will be trapped inside. Kill as few of them as possible. Concentrate on chasing them out of the area. But make sure that Lot is safe.'

There was murmured assent from the fighting men and then they went off to gather the things they would need for the journey. Servants helped them pack essential food supplies and water bottles onto their camels. They were eager for battle. For most of them it was their first.

A few days later it was over. The plan had worked perfectly. Kedorlaomer and his allies had been defeated and Abram's men chased their victims all the way to Hobah, north of Damascus. More importantly, Abram and his men had managed to rescue Lot, together with his possessions and a number of women and other prisoners.

Under the stars in the chill of the night, Abram and his nephew embraced each other warmly as victory celebrations continued, with plenty to eat and drink.

'It's good to have you back,' Abram told his nephew, warmly. But he wondered whether Lot had learned his lesson. He suspected that he hadn't. And he was right. For before long, Lot had moved back to Sodom, once again ignoring the risks.

6

A Covenant Relationship

The early morning sun began to shimmer across the beautiful valley as Abram emerged from his tent, yawned and prepared himself for another day's journey. It was some time since he and his fighting men had left Damascus to return to their wives and families. They had travelled across the Gaulau plain, down the steep ravine of the Jabbok and south by the central road to Hebron. Memories of their heroic victory were still fresh in their minds, and each night over the campfires there were animated accounts of each man's role in this triumph over Kedorlaomer and the other three kings.

News of their victory had already begun to spread throughout the region and as they continued their journey people came out to thank them for delivering them from the troublemakers who had brought death and suffering for so many years.

Later that morning, as they continued through the Valley of Shevan, they received the ultimate accolade: a double royal reception.

Abram spotted a group of men in the distance. It looked as though they were waiting for them, and as they drew nearer, Abram recognised one of them. It was the King of Sodom, the man whose reign had resulted in such corruption and immorality in that city and beyond. He was surrounded by a number of courtiers and other dignitaries. Abram smiled to himself. Maybe this wily old fellow was after his share of the spoils of war!

Standing near the King of Sodom was another man. Abram did not know him, but he was clearly someone important, judging by the way he was dressed. And there was something about him that was different from the other chiefs, kings and princes who inhabited the region.

The man approached Abram and bowed. 'My name is Melchizedek,' he said. 'I am the King of Jerusalem.' Abram returned the greeting.

'I am a priest of the Most High God,' Melchizedek continued. Abram's face lit up with delight. So he was not the only descendant of Noah in the region. He must be a link to the past age of Shem. Abram also noticed that Melchizedek called God by a name he had not heard of before: El Elyon – God Most High. That was a way of saying that the Lord was supreme above all other gods. It seemed that there was always something new to learn about him.

Melchizedek went to his camel, unloaded a goat-skin bag and brought it across to where Abram and his men were standing. The King of Sodom and his men looked on curiously. Melchizedek took out some round loaves of bread and some stone bottles containing wine.

'You and your men have performed a great service to my people,' he said with obvious gratitude. 'We have suffered for years at the hands of Kedorlaomer and his allies. Blessed be Abram by God Most High, Creator of heaven and earth. And blessed be God Most High, who delivered your enemies into your hands,' he went on.

The King of Sodom began to look most uncomfortable. He

was a worshipper of idols and had certainly never heard of this God Most High before.

'Come,' said Melchizedek. He gestured to Abram to join him in the shade of a tent that one of his servants had erected earlier. 'Let us eat and drink and celebrate God's wonderful victory.'

So the two men of God broke bread, perhaps for the first time in history, in a prophetic moment that would be repeated a million times in generations to come.

Their meal went on for some time. They had many tales to exchange about the battle, about the desert, the weather, the animals . . . and about their God. After they had finished, Abram beckoned to one of his men. 'Go to the camels carrying the goods that we plundered from Kedorlaomer's men. Count out one tenth and bring it to me.' The servant nodded and scurried off.

Later, Abram solemnly gave the goods to Melchizedek, and tithed for the first time in history.

Up to then, the King of Sodom had been resting with his court under a clump of trees, but he quickly moved closer at the sight of the gold, silver, jewellery and other precious items.

'Give me the people and keep the goods for yourself,' he said to Abram, waving towards the large group of men, women and children whom Abram and his men had released from captivity.

But Abram shook his head vigorously. He had already thought this one through. The last thing he wanted was to be in this wicked man's debt. He said to the king, 'I have raised my hand to the Lord, God Most High, Creator of heaven and earth, and have taken an oath that I will accept nothing belonging to you, not even a thread or a thong of a sandal, so that you will never be able to say, "I made Abram rich." I will accept nothing but what my men have eaten and the share that belongs to the men who went with me – to Amer, Eshcol and Mamre. Let them have their share.'

Abram was quite clear about his decision. He had made his oath before God not to have any contact with this wicked man. He was a bad influence, and Abram did not want even a hint of corruption in his life.

The king looked surprised, and very pleased. Abram had every right to keep the spoils of battle and the king certainly did not expect to have any share of them. He quickly beckoned to his servants to go and help Abram's servants to unload the goods from Abram's camels, and then an hour later set off back to Sodom. He could never have imagined the judgement God had in store for him.

Later the same day, Melchizedek hugged Abram before beginning his journey. For his part, he could never have imagined the glory God had in store for him. He arrived unannounced and disappeared from Old Testament history just as quickly. Centuries passed before it emerged that he was more than just the king of ancient Jerusalem. 'This Melchizedek was king of Salem and priest of God Most High,' the writer of the Hebrews revealed (Hebrews 7:1–3). 'Without father or mother, without genealogy, without beginning of days or end of life, like the Son of God he remains a priest for ever.'

Abram never realised that the man he sat and ate with that day was in fact God's first priest, who gave him a glimpse into the future when Jesus, the great High Priest, broke bread with his friends too.

* * *

Fight the good fight

Abram's fight with Kedorlaomer is the Bible's first recorded battle, and Abram was one of the first people in Scripture to get involved in spiritual warfare. Even though he did not have anybody to teach him, he came through victorious and has some lessons on this important subject that can help Christians today.

1. He fought for the right reasons

Abram's only motive for going to war was wanting to rescue his undeserving nephew and to end the suffering that Kedorlaomer and his allies had inflicted on the region. He did not fight for personal ambition or selfish gain. His motive for spiritual warfare was the same as ours should be: a love and concern for other people and a desire to free them from the enemy's grasp. It's easy to get dragged into warfare for the wrong reasons – the love of fighting, pride or a fascination with the world of evil. But an impure motive can result in us becoming wounded and being defeated.

2. He was willing to fight

Abram was many things – a shepherd, a tribal chief, a religious reformer, a prophet – but one thing he certainly wasn't was a warrior like David, Joshua or Caleb. His fight with Kedorlaomer was the only battle he ever fought. But he was prepared to fight when he needed to. In this respect, he was similar to Gideon, and indeed had an army of pretty much the same size. Perhaps you or I might have left the fight with Kedorlaomer to someone with a 'warfare ministry'. But we, like Abram, must be prepared to fight any battle God tells us to fight, even if warfare is not our 'gift'. Spiritual warfare is for everybody. This is why Jesus made it clear in Mark 16:17 that it was *believers* who would drive out demons, not just people with a special anointing. If we are believers, we're all called to be warriors, whether we like it or not! Clearly we will all engage the enemy in different ways and use different styles.

Some may be involved in deliverance, others might pray and others might replace the hatred in their community with love. But however we do it, we all have a part to play in the war.

3. He knew his authority

Abram suddenly changed from being the head of a clan of shepherds to someone who acted like a king, for in this region, kings were the only ones who exercised the prerogative of going to war. But Abram realised that he had royal authority to fight – an authority given by God. We too need to remember that when we go into spiritual warfare, we are kings and priests, fighting with divine authority (Mark 16:17). I remember working alongside a man with a renowned ministry in deliverance and spiritual warfare. A young Christian came up to him in awe and asked, 'Where do you get your authority from?' The man did not hesitate with his reply. 'From the Bible,' he said. 'It's there for everybody.' When we as Christians rise up and use the authority God has given us in his word, the enemy will soon begin to tremble.

4. He did not look at the odds

Humanly speaking there was no way Abram and his 318 men should have defeated Kedorlaomer and his allies. Their armies comprised highly trained troops, all fresh from winning an important battle in Sodom. Had Abram sat down and worked out his chances of success, he would have probably stayed at home and left Lot in captivity. But like Gideon, he learned that when God is on your side you are always in the majority and victory is guaranteed. We too should never look at the odds in any battle God calls us to fight. This is the mistake the Jewish spies made when they went to explore Canaan centuries later. They looked at their enemies through human eyes (Numbers 13:28–33). They saw them as giants and themselves as grasshoppers. The result was that they were beaten before they started. Had they looked at the land from God's point of view, as Joshua and Caleb did, they would have been confident of victory, no matter what the odds.

We must take care not to make the same mistake. We will always find that our enemies are bigger than we are, but they are never bigger than God. That's why we fight in Jesus' name. When we do so, we align ourselves with his victory on the cross over the powers of darkness. That will give us victory, no matter what the odds.

5. He waited for the right time to fight

King Kedorlaomer had been causing trouble in Canaan for years, but Abram left him alone, even though he was trespassing on 'his' land. He waited for the right time and the right reason to confront him. He recognised, as we should, that some enemy activity has to be left alone, either for the time being or maybe for ever. It is not admitting defeat if we cannot fight every battle. If we try to do so, we will end up weary and defeated. I find evil and enemy activity every time I step outside my front door. You probably do the same. But it's unrealistic to try and tackle it all at once. Jesus never operated a 'zero tolerance' policy with enemy activity. There were many battles he did not fight and many diseases he did not heal. It was the same for the New Testament church. We should not try to do better than they did. God's plan is to fight strategic battles that are important for the advance of his kingdom. If we concentrate on this, we will avoid needlessly wearing ourselves out.

6. He refused to compromise

Had Abram followed his cultural traditions, he would have kept the spoils of war. He had an absolute right to them. But he wanted to avoid being in the debt of the King of Sodom and he realised that it would be wrong to touch goods that belonged to his enemy. They were unclean and he did not want anything to do with them. Abram was in fact setting a standard for Joshua to follow years later, for just before Joshua's troops invaded Jericho he told them, 'Keep away from the devoted things, so that you will not bring about your own destruction by taking any of them. Otherwise you will make the camp of Israel liable to destruction and bring trouble on it' (Joshua 6:18). His soldier Achan found out the hard way that compromise can be costly, not just for yourself but for your family.

When we get involved in spiritual warfare we need to be equally aware that any kind of compromise or blurring of black and white can have terrible consequences. Although the devil is a defeated foe, he is also a legalist and knows that compromise on our part gives him the right to attack us.

7. He gave glory to God

Abram's actions after the battle show very clearly that he had no doubt as to who was behind his victory. There was no danger of success going to his head. He was full of praise to God and gave him the glory as he broke bread, tithed and joined Melchizedek in worship.

I always get worried when I hear 'spiritual warriors' making too much fuss about *their* successes and not enough of God's. God does not share his glory with anybody and we need to make sure that our 'testimonies' to God's goodness are not in fact subtle attempts to promote ourselves.

8. He was a peacemaker at heart

Abram was a man of peace. This is why he let Lot have first choice of the pastures, to avoid a quarrel. And after his victory over Kedorlaomer, you see him return to those peace-loving instincts. He could have gone to war with the King of Sodom over the spoils of war – many tribal chiefs in that region would have done so. But he broke with convention and gave the king what he did not really deserve as a way of avoiding conflict.

Jesus wants all of us to be peacemakers and told us that if we can fulfil this role, then we will be called sons of God (Matthew 5:9). That doesn't mean that we never fight. It means that when we do fight, we do so as peacemakers rather than warriors.

9. He remained teachable

It's easy to get puffed up after a few successful encounters with the enemy. It's a dangerous place to be.

But Abram, despite his triumph, was willing to learn from Melchizedek. When Melchizedek prayed in Genesis 14:19, Abram copied the language he used word for word, hearing for the first time perhaps that God was the Creator of heaven and earth. He was prepared to learn from another man and so increase his knowledge of God. We too should be prepared to learn from him and others whom God sends, sometimes unexpectedly, to teach us. If we become unteachable, defeat in battle is only just around the corner.

* * *

Abram suddenly began to feel very tired and vulnerable. He decided not to join his men as they ate and chatted round the campfire, but instead went and sat alone in his tent. He wanted to think.

Melchizedek and the King of Sodom had both been gone for several hours now and, after all the excitement of their visit, Abram began to feel a terrible sense of anticlimax. The tension and highly charged atmosphere of the last few weeks had finally begun to catch up with him. He felt exhausted.

He poked at his bowl of stew unenthusiastically and thought about his wife, Sarai. It was weeks since he had seen her and he had been so busy preparing for battle that he had hardly given her a thought. He pictured her, preparing to go to bed miles away at Mamre, and wondered if she would cry herself to sleep as she had done so many times before. He had learned to live with the stigma of barrenness, but she hadn't. It still tormented her deeply, especially when her servants and the other women muttered remarks about it behind her back.

'What if I've got it all wrong?' Abram wondered to himself. Was he really being fair to encourage her to believe God for a child when she was showing no sign of getting pregnant and was far too old to conceive? The constant disappointment was becoming harder for her to bear than the childlessness itself. Perhaps it would be kinder to tell her to forget about having children, and for him to sleep with one of his maidservants to produce an heir, like other men in the region did. The price of following God was turning out to be very high. It seemed to be all sacrifice and no reward. He was starting to lose hope.

As the sun finally set behind the mountains, those worries began to grow into agonising doubts. And the doubts developed into fear. What about Kedorlaomer and his men? What if they counter-attacked? It was quite possible. After all, this was a king who was unlikely to take a defeat lying down. What if he came after him? There was no way Abram could defeat him twice. What if they tracked him down to Mamre and attacked him at night, killing the children and taking the women? Abram began to shake, and sweat trickled down his brow and onto his beard. His thoughts were running out of control and dark fears invaded his mind.

Then it happened. It was as if someone had lit a lantern inside his gloomy tent. Abram blinked, looked around in astonishment and was consumed with a wonderful sense of peace.

He could not work out whether he was awake or asleep as a voice spoke to him through a vision: 'Do not be afraid, Abram. I am your shield, your very great reward.'

Abram knew beyond any doubt that it was God who was talking to him for the first time in years. He had come to visit him, like a friend popping round unexpectedly. Slowly he summoned the confidence to speak back to God and tell him what was on his mind.

'O Sovereign Lord,' he whispered tentatively, 'what can you give me since I remain childless and the one who will inherit my estate is Eliezer of Damascus? You have given me no children; so a servant in my household will be my heir.' He could not stop the pain and disappointment creeping into his voice.

Abram broke off suddenly. What had he said? Who was he to talk to God in this way? But the Lord replied gently, his voice full of reassurance. 'This man will not be your heir,' he said, 'but a son coming from your own body will be your heir.'

An overwhelming feeling of relief swept over Abram. God was not there to rebuke him! He suddenly felt an urge to go outside his tent. He groped his way through the darkness and stood, alone, under the vast black canopy that stretched above him in every direction. Thousands upon thousands of stars cascaded brilliantly through the heavens as far as he could see in the clear desert night.

'Look up at the heavens and count the stars – if indeed you can count them,' God continued. 'So shall your offspring be.'

Abram gasped in astonishment. There were millions of stars in the sky. How could he possibly have as many descendants as this? And yet deep inside he did not doubt that what God had said was true.

'I am the Lord, who brought you out of Ur of the Chaldees, to give you this land to take possession of it,' God continued.

Abram began to feel comfortable in the presence of his God. He realised that he had nothing to fear and that he was in fact talking to someone who was a friend. He remembered their chat over a meal all those years before. That had been a friendly conversation, and so was this. He looked down from the stars and said in a louder voice, 'How can I know that I shall gain possession of it?'

Abram's communion grew deeper as the Lord prepared to enter into a covenant with his friend. He instructed Abram to bring him a heifer, a goat and a ram, along with a dove and a young pigeon. From his vast stock of animals, Abram chose ones that were spotless and in their prime, slaughtered them and then carefully cut them in half. Then he laid the halves face to face on the ground, with a gap between them. It was becoming clear to him that God wanted him to walk between the separated halves of the dead animals in keeping with a ceremony used by local people when two parties were entering into a binding covenant. After all, he was clearly entering into a new agreement with God, and what better way to seal it? Some birds swooped down from the sky, ready to peck at the fresh meat. Abram angrily shooed them away. He was not going to let anything spoil his moment with the Lord. He learned that you need to be vigilant when God's presence is close, as these occasions can be full of distractions.

Abram was about to set light to the sacrifices when he was suddenly gripped with a dreadful, overpowering sense of depression. It was as though he were being consumed with evil, with darkness. He knelt by the altar, clutching his head in terror. Where was God? *Where was God?* He began to cry out. What was happening?

Through the desperate gloom, God's voice emerged again. 'Know for certain that your descendants will be strangers in a country not their own, and they will be enslaved and ill-treated four hundred years,' he said. 'But I will punish the nation they serve as slaves and afterwards they will come out with great possessions. You, however, will go to your fathers in peace and be buried at a good old age. In the fourth generation your descendants will come back here, for the sin of the Amorites has not yet reached its full measure.'

The gloom began to lift and Abram looked up, breathless and afraid. Shakily he got on with preparing the carcasses and was just about to light them when a flaming torch appeared out of nowhere. What was happening now? The fire dramatically ripped down the gap between the halves of the carcasses, igniting them with terrifying speed. The flames sent shadows across the grass. So God had taken the initiative and had confirmed the covenant in accordance with the local custom. Abram did not feel he could play his part by walking through the gap, too. This was not like other agreements he had entered into with tribal leaders. No, this one was entirely of God's making. The initiative was his alone.

By this time Abram's mind was reeling. What would happen next? And yet he also had an assurance, a confidence that he had never known before. Something had been sealed between himself and God that night.

* * *

Man's best friend

Their friendship had been sealed. God had made a covenant with Abram, just as he had done with Noah, centuries earlier. It was something he would do again, too, by sending his Son Jesus to herald a new covenant. It was, and still is, his way of demonstrating his total, unchanging and utterly reliable commitment of friendship to his people.

It is not really surprising that Abram went through a low

time after his victory over Kedorlaomer. It was a situation
waiting to happen. Most of us are prone to a dose of post-
ministry blues, and Abram was no exception. The devil is good
at using those twin weapons of doubt and fear – he has had
thousands of years of practice. Elijah suffered a similar
problem after his showdown with the prophets of Baal on
Mount Carmel. Spiritual warfare can be very costly.

What is comforting, though, is to see the way God helped
Abram through his crisis. Let's see how he restored his friend.

1. He called him by name

God was soon on the scene when Abram was struggling, and
his presence was very personal and intimate, just like a dad
caring for his son. He used his name, which is a sign of friendship and love. This is very reassuring for us, living in a day
when other religions and beliefs reduce God to a force, an
impersonal entity or an unapproachable deity. Our God is a
God of the one-to-one. He knows us intimately and he deals
with us individually in each situation. This is why we should
never compare his workings in our lives with the way he deals
with other people. He knows exactly how to handle us and how
to get the best out of us. His 'people management' skills are
perfect!

2. He met Abram at his point of need

Abram was struggling with two things: fear, and the fact that
he had sacrificed so much without seeing any kind of return. So
God tackled these problems straight away. He told him not to
be afraid, and then assured him that he would see a reward. He
could not have come to the point more quickly. Both problems
were resolved in a matter of seconds. This is why God's word
is described as a sword (Ephesians 6:17). It is swift and accu-
rate and far more productive than endless hours of counselling.

I sometimes hear long, waffley prophecies and compare them with the concise way God spoke to people in Scripture and wonder if they really are coming from the same source! God likes us to pray with brevity (Matthew 6:7) and usually replies in a similar manner. And I have always found that his ability to put his finger on the things that matter is both breathtaking and reliable.

3. He gave him hope

God knew that Abram needed a new injection of hope. He had spent years faithfully holding on to the seven promises given to him in Ur. So God returned to those original promises and fleshed them out with considerable detail – sufficient to see Abram through future trials and difficulties. He also made sure that Abram remembered them by using the stars in the sky as a visual aid – something he could sit and look at every night.

Sometimes people say to me, 'I'm worried that I won't hear God's voice.' And I always reply, 'Remember, God does not suffer from laryngitis! When God wants us to hear something, he is more than able to get the message across to us in a way we will not overlook.'

We should also remember that God does not always reveal everything about a situation in one go. Abram received God's promises in instalments, with each episode revealing more details about his plans. He does this so that he can develop ongoing faith and friendship with us.

4. He brought him to a place of peace

It is encouraging to see how Abram's mood changed during his encounter with God. To begin with he was afraid, but he soon reached a place where he was able to obey God's command to enter a covenant with him. His focus was firmly back on God rather than on his problems. Many of us find it hard to enter into God's presence, either on our own or in a meeting, when we are surrounded by those familiar giants of doubt and fear. Those birds of prey come and attack us, pecking away at our minds and hearts. But we are in good company. Abram had to fight through too. And for him it was not a question of gritting his teeth, putting on a fake smile and saying 'Praise the Lord anyway.' He was honest with God and spelled out his worries. As a result, God spoke to him and brought him to a place of peace rather than berate him because he was not there already. He will do the same for us. Any friendship that is not based on honesty is never going to go very far. Honesty about our weaknesses will always deepen our relationship with God far more than pretending we are fine when we are not.

5. He prepared Abram for the worst

One day God told me very clearly that despite my efforts to 'bond' my family together through endless trips to McDonald's, the only way to achieve real closeness was to endure suffering together. I wondered at the time why he told me this. A week later I found out. My family and I were plunged into a situation of terrible pain, and although it was a real struggle, we were able to face it because God had prepared us in advance. We knew that the ordeal was our opportunity to grow closer as a family – and we did. Forewarned was forearmed.

God prepared Abram and his family for the trials that lay ahead by giving him a disturbing prophetic encounter. He showed Abram his immediate future and also what lay in store for his family hundreds of years ahead. No doubt Abram passed these words down to his son, Isaac, who in turn communicated them to subsequent generations. This would have given them confidence that God was going to be with them during the hard times ahead.

Some people struggle with the idea of God bringing them bad news. Sometimes they naïvely dismiss it as a curse. But although doses of candy-floss prophecies are a lot more palatable, they are usually very unreal, lack substance and are of no help when life deals us those inevitable blows.

It is easy to get caught up with endless debates about 'if God knew that trouble was on the way, why didn't he stop it?'. There is no easy answer to this important question, but joining the debate can sidetrack us and as a result we can miss his fatherly warnings that prepare us for the future. God is the God of good news – and bad! Paul said quite clearly in Acts 20:23 that the Holy Spirit had repeatedly warned him that hardship and prison were on the agenda, and Jesus had no hesitation in telling Peter the kind of death that awaited him (John 21:18–19). Prophets who do not warn people of trials as well as blessings are not doing their job properly.

6. He responded to his worship

Imagine how amazed Abram must have been with that instant barbecue (Genesis 15:17)! I suspect that the food was cooked in seconds! I would have loved to see the look on Abram's face. But the important point is that as Abram worshipped, God responded, with fire – something that became synonymous with God's presence over the years (Exodus 13:21; 19:18). God will always respond to our worship, provided we give him the time and offer it in spirit and in truth. Sometimes he responds with fire, or maybe with power, healing or conviction. But giving him time is the key. Sadly, our personal worship tends to be crammed into our busy schedules, and our corporate worship can be fine-tuned and orchestrated to such an extent that we do not give God any chance to respond. We should make sure we allow God the opportunity to be a participant rather than a spectator.

7

A Friendship Is Sealed

The shouting and shrieking made everyone stop and look. Servants paused from their duties, exchanged nervous glances and then began work again in embarrassment. The arguing continued and became more heated. Then there was the sound of a slap, followed by the sound of crying.

Abram, who was adjusting the poles of his tent nearby, shook his head and sighed. The commotion, he thought, was no one else's fault but his own. Once again he had let God down.

The sobbing continued as Abram walked away from the tents occupied by his vast clan and went off on his own. He wanted time to think, to reflect on the last few turbulent weeks.

It had been ten years since he had first entered Canaan and Sarai was still not pregnant. Her pain was becoming unbearable. She was despondent and impatient, and the issue had started to dominate her entire thinking. Bearing children was vitally important to women in Canaan. A large family was an important status symbol, and childless couples were despised. For Sarai, barrenness was even harder to bear because God had promised Abram a son. The disappointment was overwhelming. It was easier for him, Abram mused, because he had heard God state the promise three times. Poor Sarai, on the other hand, had no choice but to rely on her husband's faith in the face of her advancing age. And after years of tormenting delay, she had finally had enough.

Matters came to a head one night after they had finished their meal, when Sarai said, right out of the blue, 'The Lord has kept me from having children. Go, sleep with my maidservant; perhaps I can build a family through her.' Abram, against his better judgement, had foolishly compromised and agreed. And that, he reflected, had been just the start of their problems. For now the maidservant, an Egyptian girl named Hagar, was pregnant, and Sarai, rather than being pleased that her plan had worked, was furious. The envy and hurt were consuming her and she had begun seriously mistreating Hagar. It had started with snide remarks but then developed into one angry confrontation after another, and now violence.

Abram sighed again and tried to justify his actions to himself. After all, he thought, God had never actually told him that Sarai was to be the mother of his child, and it was quite normal in these parts for a man to take another wife if his first wife agreed. It was also normal for the second wife to produce children for her husband if the first wife could not have them. Abram knew of men in other tribes who had done the same thing. And it was also normal practice to allow Sarai to deal with Hagar now in whatever way she felt fit. After all, Hagar was her slave and it was up to her to sort the girl out.

But deep inside, Abram knew that he was just kidding himself. He was not living by Canaanite values. He was trying to walk in God's ways, and was failing miserably again. Abram pondered his lack of faith and trust and his weaknesses in being persuaded to take matters into his own hands. His eagerness to please his wife had led to nothing but trouble.

Later that day, tears welled up in his eyes when he heard that Hagar had disappeared. She had fled the camp, presumably to try and get back to her family in Egypt. Abram thought about the harsh journey that lay ahead of her and began to realise the part he had played in her plight – possibly even her death.

There was no escaping the fact that he had betrayed his friendship with God once again.

The sun beat down mercilessly on the solitary figure staggering weakly along the barren caravan route. Hagar was close to unconsciousness. The 110-degree heat and lack of water had brought her to the point of dehydration. Death was a matter of hours away. But anger and hurt were driving her on. She had to get away. Away from Sarai. Away from Abram. Back home to her people. She clutched her stomach and bent over in agony. She had been dogged with contractions for several hours and knew that she could miscarry her baby unless she got rest and water soon. She also knew that if she sat down now, she would probably never get up again.

She shielded her eyes against the glare of the sun and scanned the horizon yet again for some signs of life, of water or shelter. But there was nothing. Or was there? She looked again. Was that a clump of palm trees in the distance? Or were her eyes playing tricks on her again? No. This was real. She drew herself up and began walking again with more determination and energy.

Less than an hour later, she was drinking desperately from the fountains at Shur, a small oasis in the middle of the desert on the west of Arabia Petraea, between Palestine and Egypt. She did not stay there long, however. The God who spoke to Abram spoke to her in the same way – only the second time in Scripture that he had spoken to a woman (Eve was the first). He called her by name and asked what she was doing. He told her what to do and gave her fresh hope in the middle of her pain. He cared about her. As a result, Hagar was soon heading back the way she had come, to an uncertain future at the hands of her unpredictable mistress. Maybe as she walked back towards Abram's household she reflected that God had never spoken to Sarai, but had taken the time to seek out someone like her – an unimportant, pregnant Egyptian slave girl who had been unwittingly caught up in another family's crisis.

A few months later, she and Abram cuddled their baby son affectionately as Sarai wept tears of anger and bitterness outside the tent.

* * *

What's your Ishmael?

Christians struggle with God's timing in important issues, possibly more than anything else. God often seems painfully and unnecessarily slow to answer our prayers and to fulfil his promises. The situation is not helped when people give us prophecies that provide times and dates when they are going to be fulfilled. Our 24-hour, instant-access society tends to make us impatient, and as a result we get hurt and disappointed when God does not show up when we think he should.

We so easily lose sight of the fact that God's timing is completely different from ours. To him a year is like a thousand days (Psalm 90:4). Work that out if you can! In our impatience and frustration, we forget that his ways are best and we take matters into our own hands, just as Abram did. The result for him was a boy called Ishmael, who caused him nothing but trouble from the day he was born. The result for us can be the same: an Ishmael.

So what is an Ishmael? Well, for us it's certainly not a person. God's heart is always to bless people if they are prepared to let him. No, an Ishmael is something we produce through our own efforts. It is the product of our flesh – something born out of impatience and striving. And because it has not been produced by faith, it is sin, for in God's sight anything that is not done in faith is sin.

Our Ishmael might be a project, a decision, a career move, a house purchase, a church plant – all kinds of things – but one thing is for certain: although it may receive some measure of blessing, just as Abram's son Ishmael did, it will never produce spiritual fruit or become God's way of fulfilling his promises. Only God's will, carried out in his way and in his time, can achieve these things.

Let's look at some of the other qualities of an Ishmael.

1. Ishmael is the result of a weak character and a breakdown in trust

Abram fathered his Ishmael because, just like Adam, he was not strong enough to say no to his wife and did not trust God sufficiently to fulfil his promises when the chips were down. He bowed to Sarai's pain and frustration rather than believe God's word. Sarai was quite clear that God was to blame for her barren condition (Genesis 16:2), and maybe he was, but Abram compromised rather than encourage her to carry on trusting God. His faith was tested within his own household, and was found lacking.

2. Ishmael is the result of taking God's will into our own hands

If we are honest, most of us are quite capable of living a 'Christian' life without any help from God at all. We can answer our own prayers and bring about God's promises if we put our minds to it. We have the ingenuity and the resources to do a lot of his work for him. We pray for extra money, and then get a bigger overdraft or a loan. Now there is nothing wrong with playing our part in achieving God's will, but the questions we need to ask ourselves are: Are we acting in faith? Are we acting on God's say-so? If the answer to either of these questions is no, then we are simply acting according to our flesh and will reap the consequences: an Ishmael.

3. Ishmael involves mistreating other people

We rarely conceive an Ishmael by ourselves. If we are trying to force God's will in a situation, we usually need other people's help, or at least their tacit agreement. Getting it might be difficult, especially if they are more patient and spiritually switched on than we are, so we end up persuading, manipulating or forcing them into co-operating with our plans. We need to beware pressuring other people into doing things and to stand firm if they try to do the same with us. God's will is never achieved through manipulation, threats or pressure, and whenever you see these things, you can be pretty sure that an Ishmael is being hatched somewhere.

4. Ishmael involves lust, not love

Love can always wait – it is patient (1 Corinthians 13:4). Lust wants its own way, straight away. If we are not prepared to wait for God in a situation, are forcing an issue, or are demanding that something is done *now*, then the chances are that God is not involved. I remember a man I knew wanting to initiate a new project in church. The leaders said no, so he took things into his own hands, and went ahead with it anyway. The results were devastating, especially for him and his family. The mere fact that he was not prepared to wait and submit his plans to other people demonstrated that God was not involved. He paid a high price for his impatience. The project haunted him for years and caused nothing but trouble, not only for him but for everyone else who became involved in it. Nothing seemed to work, no matter what was tried, and even when he abandoned the project, it still seemed to maintain a life of its own, generating an aftermath of debt, bad feeling, confusion and hurt.

This is because Ishmaels are conceived by sowing a huge amount of fleshly activity. And that is what you reap.

5. Ishmael will not bring about God's promises

The terrible thing about an Ishmael is that it will never bear spiritual fruit. It can't, for that which is flesh remains flesh, and that which is spirit remains spirit (Galatians 4:29). The two are in permanent conflict with one another (Galatians 5:17–18). Although we might argue that our Ishmael is in fact the fulfilment of God's promise, it never can be and never will be. God may, in his mercy, continue to fulfil his original promise anyway – as he did by giving Isaac to Abram and Sarai – but if he does so, it will be as well as Ishmael, not instead of! As Abram and Sarai found, living with both can be troublesome and complicated.

6. Ishmael causes trouble and division

God was quite clear to Hagar what Ishmael would be like (Genesis 16:12): wild, offensive, hostile, with everyone against him. It might sound as though the poor boy was cursed by God before he was born, but his character was nothing to do with God. It was the result of his conception – of the things that had been sown into his life by Abram and Hagar.

- They sowed in the flesh, and Ishmael grew up into a man who was controlled by his flesh.
- They sowed from a place of division and family strife, and Ishmael was someone who caused division and strife.
- They sowed independently from God, and Ishmael became independent.
- They sowed by abandoning God, and Ishmael later abandoned God and went to live in idolatrous Egypt.

Our Ishmaels will do all these things too. The projects, plans, decisions and agendas that are the result of our impatience and lack of trust in God will inevitably damage our families and others in the body of Christ. They are incapable of doing anything else, because all the wrong things have been sown into them.

We must heed the warning: taking God's will into our own hands is dangerous, and the consequences can ruin our lives and those of others.

Before we act on God's promises, we must ask ourselves, and other people: Are we acting in human effort, or in God's strength? Are we being driven by haste, or led in peace? Are we breaking down doors, or seeing God open them? Are we causing division and steamrollering others, or working in unity with them? Are we forcing the issue by borrowing money to pay for the project, or seeing God provide for our needs? Are we twisting God's arm, or letting him lead us?

Be warned: if you are in the process of conceiving an Ishmael, then stop now, before it is too late.

* * *

The camp was strangely quiet apart from the occasional groan from one of the men inside their tents. Women exchanged furtive, embarrassed smiles and then got on with their jobs. Here and there, spots of blood congealed in the sunshine.

Over the previous few days, the men in Abram's clan – hundreds of them – had just endured the embarrassment and agony of being circumcised with a rough flint knife. And it hurt! Some were unable to walk because of the pain.

Some of the men had found the ritual hard to understand. They had heard about other nations performing it – circumcision was by no means uncommon – but what had surprised them was that Abram had insisted that *every* male had to be done, regardless of their age or status. Slaves, boys and even babies over eight days old were all included. This was unusual. But Abram was quite clear about it: God had spoken and had to be obeyed straight away. He had then set an example by having himself and Ishmael done the same day. Anyone who refused to undergo the rite would be expelled from his clan immediately. The choice was theirs. But none of them said no. They were beginning to understand that circumcision was God's way of setting them apart from all other tribes and clans by marking their flesh in a distinct and irreversible manner.

God had given his instructions about the ceremony in yet another encounter with his friend Abram. It was the first time for 13 years that he had spoken to Abram directly. Maybe the silence reflected God's sadness over the way Abram had compromised and mistreated Hagar. As ever, the Lord's appearance had caught Abram by surprise and he fell flat on his face, the greatest gesture of respect and reverence he knew.

God had gone on to reiterate his original promises to Abram: promises about having a child, which made Abram laugh, and about inheriting Canaan. But this time he went further. He had not only told Abram about circumcision, he had also guaranteed that his covenant to Abram would last for ever. He told him that Abram's long-promised son would arrive within a year and that he should call him Isaac. He promised him that he would be the God of the nation that Abram was going to father, and he told Abram that he wanted to change his name to Abraham (father of many) and Sarai's to Sarah (princess), as a prophetic illustration of the people they were to become.

* * *

So it was another life-changing encounter – a conversation bursting with vision, promise and hope. It was also one that showed how much further Abram had gone in developing his friendship with God, for God gave Abram more detail about his plans than he had ever done before. This was because Abram was beginning to prove himself capable of coping with the finer detail. He had been following God for many decades and the struggles and blessings had developed his character so that he was mature enough to handle more revelation. God always knows how much to tell us about each situation, and we need to understand that he knows best at those times when we are frustrated by his lack of detail.

The conversation also shows that Abram had become very relaxed in God's presence – relaxed enough to laugh, to joke about God's word under his breath and then even exchange a quip with him about having a child in old age. Laughing and joking together are always signs of real friendship, but with Abram that did not mean he had become over-familiar with his Lord. The reverence was still there. That was why Abram fell to the ground when God first appeared to him. He had a wonderful balance in his relationship that we can learn from. It's easy to be either over-familiar with God or so reverent that we never experience an intimate friendship with him. He wants us to experience both, as Abram did.

A strange request

Some people find it hard to understand why God insisted on his people being circumcised. What was the point of such a barbaric and almost bizarre ceremony? In fact circumcision gives us some wonderful insights into God's heart towards friendship. Let's have a look at them.

1. Circumcision shows that friendship costs something

I remember once listening to the Argentinian evangelist Luis Pulau rebuking a British congregation. 'The trouble with you

English', he said, 'is that you have no commitment in your friendships. You are very close to people one day, and then you move away, lose touch and never speak to them again.' He had a point. In our church culture, friends can be like disposable razor blades – when they start to hurt, you simply get another one. Ask yourself this question: How many of the friends you had ten years ago are still your friends now? Possibly none. Those people whom you loved, ate with, prayed with and cried with are nowhere today. They hurt you. They got another job and you lost touch. How sad. And how unlike the loyal, lasting friendships that God wants us to have with him and other people. Unfortunately, if we mistreat or lose touch with our human friends, the chances are that we will treat God in the same way.

The fact that he wanted to seal his covenant with Abram with circumcision spells out one thing loud and clear: friendship with him means being prepared to shed blood, to endure pain in your most sensitive places and to bear life-long scars. Jesus did all this for us when he demonstrated his friendship to the whole human race by dying on the cross. Being God's friend is wonderful, a privilege beyond imagination. But it is not something you rush into. It can hurt. It involves sacrifice. This is why God told Abram it was a covenant in his flesh. Friendship with God certainly isn't disposable, and if we begin to understand what that friendship with him entails, our attitude to our human friends will never be the same again.

2. Circumcision shows that friendship goes two ways

If a friendship is one way, eventually it will fail. I remember trying to befriend a couple once. We had them round for dinner, took loads of initiatives and tried to pop in and see them whenever we could. But although they were polite enough, it became apparent after a while that they did not really want to know. So the friendship eventually failed. And they were not in the wrong, for Scripture makes it quite clear (Amos 3:3) that you cannot walk in friendship with people unless you both agree. You cannot make people be your friends if they don't want to be. Jesus tried to befriend Judas, but no amount of love ever persuaded him to return the gesture. Friendship in church is *not* compulsory! Love, however, is – the Bible commands it (John 13:34).

When God unveiled his covenant of friendship to Abram, he made it clear that it was a two-way arrangement. He would be God, a friend, to Abram's descendants, provided they were circumcised. But if they refused to comply, then they would be cut off, not just from him but from the rest of God's people too. It was as simple as that. God made it clear that friendship with him involves both blessings and obedience. You cannot have one without the other. The same still applies today.

3. Circumcision shows that friendship comes from a love relationship

If the love goes out of a marriage, all you have left is a meaningless piece of paper, a certificate. The certificate might say that you are legally married, but if you and your partner cannot stand one another, it is pointless. You can put it in a gold frame and mount it on the wall, but that won't change a thing, for God is interested in reality, not in outward signs that are nothing more than a cover-up.

When he told Abram about circumcision, he made it clear that the ritual was only a *sign* of obedience. It meant nothing in itself. This is why Paul wrote to the Romans hundreds of years later, 'Circumcision has value if you observe the law, but if you break the law, you have become as though you had not been circumcised . . . A man is not a Jew if he is only one outwardly, nor is circumcision merely outward and physical. No, a man is a Jew if he is one inwardly; and circumcision is circumcision of the heart, by the Spirit . . .' (2:25, 28–29).

God was looking for a heart relationship with Abram and his people, and circumcision was to be a *sign* of that friendship. Similarly, he is looking for a heart relationship with us. Outward signs – baptism, going to church on Sundays, speaking in tongues or praying impressive prayers – mean nothing if they do not convey what is really going on inside us. If our outward behaviour towards God is different from what is in our hearts, then we need to go to him and begin to build an honest relationship.

4. *Circumcision shows that friendship with God is based on equality among believers*

As far as we know, Abram's household was the first in history where every male underwent circumcision. And to this day the Jewish race is the only one that insists on circumcision for every male. Although the ritual has always been practised by many tribes and religions throughout the world, it has never been something for all men. This is because God wanted everyone, both men and women, to enjoy that covenant friendship with him. There were no exclusions and no favourites. If we decide to enter into that covenant, we become just like everyone else. It doesn't matter if people are richer than we are, better than we are or more important than we are. It doesn't matter if they are apostles and we just give out the hymn books at the church door. In God's eyes, they are the same as us. This is why Jesus' brother James is so clear in forbidding favouritism in James 2. From God's point of view, if we bear the scars of circumcision, then we are his friends, and stand on level ground with all of God's saints.

5. *Circumcision shows that friendship can only come with a change of heart*

There are some people with whom you just don't feel comfortable. You try to love them, but they are abrasive, rude, critical or unkind. It is very hard to relate to them. They need to change if they want to make any real friends.

It is the same for God. He loves us, but we will never develop friendship with him if he does not feel comfortable with us. So he gets to work to make us the kind of people he can relate to. This is what he did with Abram. He took him through years of trials and difficulties to bring him to maturity. And Abram got there in the end.

Thankfully we Christians do not have to undergo physical circumcision, but this does not mean that we escape the pain! God wants to establish friendship with us by having our hearts circumcised (Romans 2:29). Circumcision is always done by someone else. So the reality of sealing that friendship with God means having other people cutting us to the heart with their words and actions. Ouch! Yes, it will hurt us. It is what church life is all about. Other believers will use us, abuse us, let us down, gossip about us and lie to us. They will really get to us! But God's agenda behind all this is to deal with our pride, our love of ourselves, our selfishness and our determination to do things our own way. When we have died to these things, we can be confident that God will feel more comfortable with us and will be able to offer us his friendship as well as love. Sadly, God has far more believers than friends. And as Abram discovered later on, friends are the ones whom God really listens to when there is important business to be discussed.

8

A Woman in Need

Sarah's hand gripped the bowl so tightly that her knuckles turned white, and she reached across the table and snatched a spoon, her actions tense and deliberate. Then she began stirring the mixture, faster and faster. As she did so she gritted her teeth and muttered angrily under her breath. Suddenly, in a fit of pent-up rage, she hurled the bowl across the tent. A slave girl nearby ducked, gasped with fright and scurried outside. Moments later came the sound of wailing – the deep, heart-rending cries of a woman still tormented by barrenness and broken-hearted with disappointment.

But her pain brought an immediate response from heaven.

The following day was just like any other in Abraham's settlement in Mamre. The men were out tending the animals while the women prepared a meal, helped by the young girls. Sarah was still sulking inside her tent. She had refused to come out since the incident the day before, and nobody dared go near her.

Abraham reached out for a bottle and sipped some water. He looked up at the sun, now high in the sky. It must be the middle of the day, he thought. Time for a rest. He was just preparing to lie down when he noticed three men standing a few yards away. He wondered why he had not noticed them before. He quickly rose from his mat and walked towards them, shrewdly weighing them up in the tradition of all desert-dwellers. Abraham noted their grand clothes and the air of authority they carried with them. They must be important tribal chiefs or kings, he thought. He was surprised he did not recognise them. After all, he knew most of the rulers in the region. But custom prevented him from asking who they were, where they were from or where they were going.

Abraham bowed down low to the ground – the most respectful greeting he could offer. Normally a tribal chief like himself would merely stand to greet a stranger, but these were obviously no ordinary visitors. The men acknowledged his greeting.

Abraham stood up again and said to the three men, 'If I have found favour in your eyes, my lord, do not pass your servant by. Let a little water be brought, and then you may all wash your feet and rest under this tree. Let me get you something to eat, so you can be refreshed and then go on your way – now that you have come to your servant.'

'Very well,' the men answered, 'do as you say.'

Abraham was typical of men in that region. They always offered hospitality to passers-by and would be offended if it were refused. Abraham was mindful of the fact that the men had probably been travelling for several hours by now. People in those parts always began their journeys before sunrise and then stopped for a rest at midday, when the sun was at its hottest.

Abraham hurried into the tent to Sarah. 'Quick,' he said, 'get three seahs of fine flour and knead it and bake some bread.'

Sarah grunted a disinterested acknowledgement. The last thing she wanted to do right now was entertain visitors. But she grudgingly got on with the task, mixing the flour with some water, kneading it into round cakes and then baking them on the camel-dung fire.

Abraham ran to his herd and selected one of his best calves and gave it to a servant with orders to slaughter it and cut it up, ready to cook. The servant looked surprised. It was rare to offer strangers meat. Important ones might perhaps be offered a lamb or a young goat, but certainly not a calf. These guests must be very significant.

After a while the meal was ready and Abraham presented it to his guests, who accepted it gratefully. He went and stood nearby under a huge tree. Even though he had servants available to wait on the guests, he honoured them by standing by them as they ate, ready to attend their needs personally.

After the meal, the man who appeared to be the leader of the three said to Abraham, 'Where is your wife Sarah?'

'There in the tent,' he replied. And as the words left his lips, a thought struck him like a thunderbolt: the man had called Sarah by her new name – the one given to her a few days earlier by God. Not even all the people in Abraham's clan knew her new name. How could these men know it if they had never met her before? God himself was the only one who knew. The colour drained from Abraham's cheeks as he suddenly realised that the man sitting talking to him was probably God himself. His mind went back to the stranger who had passed through and spoken to him at Shechem all those years ago. Yes, his bearing was now vaguely familiar.

The man broke into Abraham's trance-like state. 'I will surely return to you about this time next year, and Sarah your wife will have a son,' he said.

Sarah was still inside the tent, as women in her culture were not allowed to eat with men, but she nonetheless heard the words clearly. She too wondered how the man knew her name and was pondering the subject when she heard him talk about her having a son. Immediately her face hardened and she laughed to herself. 'After I am worn out and my master is old, will I now have this pleasure?' she muttered to herself with a mocking sneer.

Outside in the sunshine, the man – the Lord – spoke to Abraham reprovingly: 'Why did Sarah laugh and say, "Will I really have a child, now that I am old?"? Is anything too hard for the Lord?' Abraham looked down in embarrassment. He was still struggling to come to terms with the fact that God himself was sitting there, enjoying his food and talking to him. Being rebuked, even gently, by him was hard to take.

The Lord resumed, 'I will return to you at the appointed time next year and Sarah will have a son.'

Sarah peered nervously round the tent door. She was shaking with fear. Somehow she knew this was no ordinary stranger. How did he know she had laughed? After all, she had not laughed out loud. She feared a telling off and so decided to lie about it. 'I did not laugh,' she said to the man hesitantly.

The man looked up at her, not with anger but with eyes that were full of love and understanding. 'Yes, you did laugh,' he said. And as he finished the sentence, Sarah felt an inner peace that she had not known before. Somehow she knew that what the man had said about her bearing a son was right. She went back inside the tent and wept again, but this time they were tears of joy. She had encountered God for herself now. It was easier to believe him once you had met him.

* * *

You find examples of God's love for people on every page of Scripture, but his encounter with Sarah must be one of the most moving. It shows his kindness in a wonderful way.

Sarah was a woman at breaking point. Other women who

have been childless will understand only too well how she felt:
the pain, the doubts about their femininity, the sense of failure,
the feeling of disapproval by God, the harsh words of other
people, the disappointment month by month at discovering that
conception has still not happened. No wonder Sarah began to
grow hard.

Some people would have expected God to be angry with
her. But he wasn't. Quite the opposite in fact. He saw her
despair, and rather than rebuke her he did something about it.
He summoned two angels and left heaven especially to help
her.

Let's be clear: the main reason the Lord called that day was
out of concern for Sarah. Yes, he also had business to do with
Abraham about Sodom and Gomorrah, but that could wait.
Sarah's well being came first. She needed a visit.

It is easy to assume that when the Lord called by with his
angels, he only came to see Abraham. After all, most of the
ensuing conversation did not involve Sarah. But remember,
God had already told Abraham a few days earlier that Isaac
would be born the following year. Abraham did not need to
hear the promise again. No, the Lord repeated it just for Sarah's
benefit. He knew she was listening and also knew that custom
prevented her from joining the men for their meal. So he told
Abraham about Isaac again so that she could hear the promise
for herself. God also needed to make sure that Sarah knew it
was he, the Lord, who was speaking, so he used her new name
to catch her attention, just as it did Abraham's. And to empha-
sise the point, he reproached her for lying, not because he was
angry, but to demonstrate his supernatural knowledge. Sarah
had laughed to herself, privately inside the tent. The men
outside should not have known anything about it.

I am quite sure that after God left, Sarah never doubted that
the Lord had spoken to her. And as he walked off with her

husband and the two angels, she probably marvelled at the God who was prepared to leave heaven to come and comfort a suffering shepherd woman. It shows so much about his compassion.

If you are struggling with childlessness, or anything else, you will find that God will have the same compassion for you. He will see past your depression to the pain in your heart, and he will bring healing.

The fact that God showed up personally to have lunch with Abraham also shows the depth of their friendship. Do you sometimes pop round to your friend's house for a meal? Well, God does the same! Once he had seen that Abraham was prepared to obey his commands about circumcision, he knew that their relationship had come to the point where a meal and a chat were in order. He felt comfortable in Abraham's company and knew that Abraham felt the same about him.

We too will find that obedience will result in deeper friendship with God. When he sees that we can be trusted, he will take initiatives to develop the relationship. Maybe we, like Abraham, will end up with angels calling round for a snack (Hebrews 13:2).

* * *

The guests rose to their feet. It was time to go. Desert custom dictated that they could remain for three-and-a-half days, but they had other things to do. Abraham quickly joined them and escorted them out of the camp to see them on their way. After a short walk they came to a place called Caphar Barucha, where the Dead Sea and the town of Sodom were visible through a ravine. They stopped and gazed at the scene before them: a breathtaking view across the Jordan plain with terraced vineyards, palm groves and fruit trees growing dates, oranges and bananas, and the shimmering waters of the Dead Sea in the distance.

Abraham was about to return to his tent when the Lord took him by surprise again. 'The outcry against Sodom and Gomorrah is so great', he said, 'and their sin so grievous that I will go down and see if what they have done is as bad as the outcry that has reached me. If not, I will know.' The words startled Abraham and he immediately thought about his nephew Lot and his family. What about them?

What he did not realise was that God wanted to involve him in the decision about the future of these two cities. He surmised that his friendship with Abraham was at the point where he could reveal his intentions and discuss the issue with him.

Abraham, relaxed after entertaining the Lord for lunch, felt confident enough to put his views to him. Summoning the courage, he almost blurted out, 'Will you sweep away the righteous with the wicked? What if there are fifty righteous people in the city? Will you really sweep it away and not spare the place for the sake of the fifty righteous people in it?' Abraham paused for a moment, his heart pounding. He could scarcely believe what he was doing. Taking a deep breath, he continued as the Lord listened intently. 'Far be it from you to do such a thing – to kill the righteous with the wicked, treating the righteous and the wicked alike. Far be it from you! Will not the Judge of all the earth do right?'

He stopped and waited for the Lord's reply. Part of him feared a rebuke. But no, he knew his God better than that. And he was right. The Lord said, 'If I find fifty righteous people in the city of Sodom, I will spare the whole place for their sake.'

And so the conversation continued: two friends discussing events that shaped history. Abraham spoke up again. 'Now that I have been so bold as to speak to the Lord, though I am nothing but dust and ashes, what if the number of righteous people is five less than fifty? Will you destroy the whole city because of five people?'

'If I find forty-five there,' he said, 'I will not destroy it.'

Once again Abraham spoke to the Lord. 'What if forty are found there?'

He said, 'For the sake of forty, I will not do it.'

Then Abraham said, 'May the Lord not be angry, but let me speak. What if only thirty can be found there?'

He answered, 'I will not do it if I find thirty there.'

Abraham said, 'Now that I have been so bold as to speak to the Lord, what if only twenty can be found there?'

He said, 'For the sake of twenty, I will not do it.'

Then he said, 'May the Lord not be angry, but let me speak just once more. What if only ten can be found there?'

He said, 'For the sake of ten, I will not destroy it.'

Later on, Abraham returned to his tent, hoping that he had done enough to save the city. He had a feeling he had not.

A while later, Abraham returned to his tent and sat in silence, reflecting on what had been the most amazing day of his life. The Lord had gone off to examine Sodom and Gomorrah, to see if he could find ten righteous people there. Abraham knew that his chances of doing so were slim and that his fumbling intercession might not have been enough to avert impending doom. Once again he thought about Lot and his family and shook his head with worry.

*　*　*

The conversation between God and Abraham that day must be one of the most remarkable instances of intercession that has ever taken place. It gives some amazing insights into the Lord's character. The mere fact that he wanted to hear Abraham's opinions about his plan to bring judgement on Sodom and Gomorrah shows him to be a God of humility. It also shows him to be a God who cares about his friendships.

There are many books and videos that provide techniques

and methods for prayer. Some are helpful, but many miss out the most important element: that the key to effective prayer is having a deep friendship with God. If this exists, it does not matter which formula you use, since you can be confident that God always listens to his friends and responds to them, just as he did with Abraham. Abraham's approach with God that day was nothing particularly clever. It bore more resemblance to bartering in a market than praying in some great super-spiritual way. It was bold and definite.

Many people try to read great spiritual mysteries into the conversation. To do so misses the point. It was not some heaven-bursting ministry of intercession. It was simply a chat between two close friends in which Abraham and God spoke six times each. It certainly was not a monologue, which intercession can be. Abraham almost became foolish towards the end of the conversation, trying to drive the numbers ever downwards. But the words touched God's heart because they were spoken by his friend. Had you or I uttered them, they may not have been acknowledged in the same way.

Abraham's intercession – more personal than any other recorded in Scripture – was not based on a smart technique. It was not based on his ability to pray. It was based on a friendship that had developed over many years. As Jesus explained to his disciples many years later, 'You are my friends if you do what I command. I no longer call you servants, because a servant does not know his master's business. Instead, I have called you friends' (John 15:14–15).

I'm not a gifted intercessor and I find prayer difficult. My mind wanders so much I often forget what I am praying about! But the only way I will ever improve is to strengthen my friendship with God. No technique on earth will ever make God listen if my friendship is not there in the first place.

What makes an intercessor?

There were other keys (rather than methods) to Abraham's success in intercession that day. Let's look at them.

1. Abraham had proved his faithfulness

Abraham certainly made his mistakes, and he continued to make them until the day he died, just as we all do. He was no super-saint, but he had the quality that God always looks for: faithfulness. He persevered with God's call through difficult circumstances over many decades and proved to God that he was a loyal friend – not someone who would quit under pressure. He sometimes went years without God speaking to him at all, and yet still did not weaken in his faith. This is why his opinions mattered to God. They were worth hearing. Ask yourself whose opinions you would listen to: those of a long-standing, trusted friend, or those of someone who dips in and out of your friendship, saying they love you one day and then ignoring you the next. I expect your answer would be the same as God's. The best way to improve your prayer life is to improve your loyalty and faithfulness to him. In time he will share with you the deep things that are on his heart (1 Corinthians 2:10).

The easy access that the blood of Jesus gives us to God's throne may lead us to assume that just because we can approach him with boldness and confidence (Hebrews 4:16), it naturally follows that he will listen to us and answer all our prayers. This is not necessarily the case, and using any number of 'name it and claim it' verses will not twist God's arm or change the situation! This does not mean that we should not boldly claim God's promises written in Scripture. But the key is to claim them as a result of our friendship with him. God is most likely to listen to the prayers of his friends – people who are trustworthy and who have clean hands and pure hearts (Psalm 24:4).

2. Abraham had learned to love people

If we spend time in the company of a good person, we end up taking on some of their nicer characteristics, such as kindness, gentleness and a positive attitude. Abraham had spent a lot of time in God's presence over many years and as a result had become more and more like his Lord. So when he was interceding for Sodom and Gomorrah, his instincts, like God's, were to show mercy and to find a way of avoiding destruction. Abraham had learned the divine principle of mercy triumphing over judgement – an important one for any of us who want to intercede effectively.

Centuries later, Jonah showed that he had not grasped this principle. He wanted God to wipe out the wicked people of Nineveh, and he was deeply offended when God showed them kindness instead. Jonah's lack of mercy eventually hindered his prayers and his relationship with God. He might have had a great anointing as a prophet, but he did not have God's love for people.

3. Abraham was confident and relaxed in God's presence

I remember once having to go to a lunch attended by the Queen Mother. I have never been so scared in my life! I spent days worrying about it and then sat through the entire meal feeling sick with anxiety and feeling distinctly uncomfortable in the presence of such a grand lady. How then would I respond if God turned up for dinner one day? I think I would die of fright, and I certainly would not feel very relaxed as he asked me to pass the tomato ketchup and offered me the last slice of pizza. How sad! This reaction shows that I do not know God particularly well and that my friendship with him does not go very deep. If it did, I would be reverent but relaxed, as Abraham was. Although Abraham was probably amazed by God's visit that day, he was certainly not overwhelmed by it. He was able to show warmth and respect and conversed with God quite easily and confidently, because his friendship with God had become strong and secure. And this friendship provided the basis for effective intercession.

4. Abraham knew that God was someone who answered prayer

God's visit to Abraham came at a time when Abraham was strong in his faith. After all, he had just entered into a covenant relationship with the Lord, and God had recently told him that Isaac would be born within a year, after decades of delay. This patient waiting had taught him that God does answer prayer if you give him time. This would have given him confidence that God would hear his cries for Sodom and Gomorrah and act on them if he could.

5. Abraham knew that God cared about the things he cared about

My six-year-old boy Jacob cares a lot about the tent he got for his birthday. As a result, so do I. I care about the things Jacob cares about because I love him. It's the same with God. He cares about the things you care about, just as he cared about the things Abraham cared about. He understood that Abraham would be concerned about Lot if judgement fell upon Sodom, so he took the time and trouble to find Abraham, to tell him his plans and listen to Abraham's opinions. He took them on board, too, by making sure that Lot's life was spared. That's what I call caring!

6. Abraham knew God's character

Good friends are close enough to know how the other will

respond in different situations. My wife knows me well enough to be confident that if I am faced with a difficult decision, I will do precisely nothing!

By this time in Abraham's life, he knew God well enough to be confident that he was kind and loving. So when God hinted at bringing judgement upon Sodom and Gomorrah, Abraham was surprised. He had not experienced God's judgement before, other than when he witnessed the way he dealt with Pharaoh in Egypt. So Abraham said to the Lord, 'Far be it from you . . .' In other words, he was saying, 'Hey, it's not like you to do that!' And to an extent he was right. He knew that God was slow to anger and always quick to show mercy, just as he had been when Abram lied to Pharaoh about Sarai being his sister.

However, Abraham was learning more about his friend, the Lord God. He was learning that he was a God who could not let sin go unnoticed and needed to deal with the wickedness in Sodom and Gomorrah, providing that there was sufficient evidence and the opportunity given for intercession and repentance.

As we develop our friendship with God, we will discover more about his character, and this will help us to see things from his point of view when we intercede.

* * *

Abraham lifted himself off his bed, stood up, stretched wearily and rubbed his eyes. He had not slept at all, not after yesterday.

He reflected for a moment and shuddered. He had never experienced anything like it. It had started with an eerie stillness, just after dawn. Then he and his shepherds had noticed that the animals were becoming agitated and nervous. Uneasiness descended over the camp and people went about their jobs with unusual quietness. Then it happened. First a massive storm, with brilliant flashes of silver lightning ripping across the sky and awful crashes of thunder, louder than anything Abraham had ever heard before – ear-shattering, shocking detonation. Then the earth began to tremble and shake, and the lightning intensified to the point where fireballs cascaded out of the sky.

The terrible inferno raged for what seemed ages, and then . . . stillness. Not a peaceful stillness, but a disturbing, chilling calm. Not even the birds sang. And as the day wore on, the nauseous stench of sulphur began to waft across the plains.

Abraham shuddered again. The storm had been God's judgement on Sodom and Gomorrah. The Lord had obviously been to the town as promised and had found it was as bad as he had been told. Worse still, he had not been able to find ten righteousness people. So judgement had been inevitable.

Thoughts about Lot and his family crowded into Abraham's mind. Had they perished in the inferno? Abraham felt deeply troubled. If only he had left Lot in Ur! Abraham had hoped that getting the Lord to agree to withhold judgement for the sake of ten righteous people would be a way of saving his family. He had counted on Lot having brought up his daughters, sons-in-law and other family members in God's ways, so that between them they could muster ten. But clearly this was not the case. The evils of Sodom had obviously enticed Lot's family as well. Shaking his head, Abraham left his tent and decided he would go and look at the scene for himself.

Picking up his staff, he retraced the steps he had taken with the Lord and his angels just 24 hours earlier, wrinkling his nose at the smell of sulphur that still hung in the air.

After a while he came to Caphar Barucha and looked through the ravine to the valley below. He stopped and gasped. All that could be seen were thick black clouds of dense smoke hanging over the area where Sodom and Gomorrah had been situated. It looked like a scene from a furnace. Tears began to trickle down Abraham's face and onto his grey beard, as again he thought about his nephew.

Just over an hour later, Abraham walked shakily back to his tent and sat down, reflecting once again on the God who had brought about this terrible punishment. This was the same God who had become his friend, who had sat and eaten dinner with him just the day before! Up to now he had thought he was getting to know the Lord quite well, but this fierce outpouring of judgement made him realise there was a side to his friend he had never seen before. An awesome, reverent fear touched his heart and he vowed to himself to walk righteously before God in future. The destruction of Sodom and Gomorrah had taught him a lesson he would never forget. Or would he? Perhaps not. Time alone would tell.

It was only later that he heard God had spared Lot and his children by allowing them to flee to the nearby town of Zoar just before sunrise on that dreadful day. But Lot's wife perished after disobeying God's instruction not to look back as she made her escape. She allowed herself one lingering glance at the town and its evil enticements, and it cost her her life. And even this tragedy did not make any lasting impression on Lot's heart. It was not long before he was back in sin. This time it was incest. His daughters got him drunk and he slept with them, getting them both pregnant. Sodom certainly left its mark on his family. Maybe he should have stayed in Ur after all.

* * *

What Abraham probably did not realise was that it would be a lesson that history would not forget either. God's vengeance on Sodom and Gomorrah's wickedness is still spoken about today and is referred to as a warning three times in Scripture (Deuteronomy 29:23; Isaiah 13:19; Jude 7). Evidence of that terrible day still exists in the region to haunt the sceptic and unbeliever – wells of liquid bitumen, fragments of sulphur lying on the plains and along the shores of the Dead Sea and the terrible sense of death that still hangs in the air.

Sadly, however, although history remembered, it did not learn. And neither did Abraham, who did not take long to get back into sin again.

* * *

The man looked up from filling some water skins from a well and gazed in open-mouthed admiration. The woman, meanwhile, deliberately turned her head in the opposite direction. The man smiled – a leering, seductive smile that meant only one thing. Then he walked nearer to the woman to try and attract her attention. She was beautiful – radiant, with fine features, an attractive figure and a fair complexion. Again the woman shunned him. But this man was persistent, which was unusual in a culture where a man risked serious trouble if he made any kind of approach to a woman without permission. He followed her from a discreet distance, but not for long. Suddenly there was an angry shout and an older man walked up to him purposefully.

'Leave her alone,' he said. The man hesitated. The other man raised his staff in rage. 'Be gone!' he shouted. Abraham did not take kindly to other men even looking at his wife. Three of his servants came and stood near him, ready to deal with trouble if necessary. The man backed away, muttering under his breath, and went back to tending his camels. Abraham, however, was still white with anger and fear.

It had been several months since his tribe had left Mamre and journeyed south to the district of Palestine known as the Negev. The pastures at Mamre were becoming scarce, and Abraham was finding it too painful to stay there any longer. The memories of God's destruction of Sodom and Gomorrah were still fresh in his mind and he found it disturbing to remain there. So his household struck camp for the first time in many years and took the caravan route between central Canaan and Egypt, finally settling in an area situated between Kadesh and Shur.

Because they did not know the region, Abraham decided to stay for a while in the capital city, Gerar, situated on the banks of a river and near the mouth of the huge wadi es-Sheriah. And that had been the start of their troubles.

Abraham became increasingly tormented with the fears that had plagued him in Egypt 30 years earlier. What if the people of Gerar killed him to get hold of Sarah? After a brief struggle with his conscience, he decided to resort to the same ruse that he had used with Pharaoh. He would pass her off as his sister. After all, that's what he had decided to do all those years ago, so why change?

But the plan backfired, just as it had done in Egypt. Abimelech, the King of Gerar, inevitably heard about Sarah's beauty and took her into his courts to become his wife, mindful that forming an alliance with a rich and powerful man like Abraham would no doubt serve him well in the future.

However, God had other ideas. He brought the issue to light by inflicting every woman in Abimelech's household with barrenness, and then he exposed Abraham's lies by telling Abimelech about them in a dream. Abimelech was furious and summoned Abraham into his presence.

'What have you done to us?' he demanded. 'How have I wronged you that you have brought such great guilt upon me and my kingdom? You have done things to me that should not be done. What was your reason for doing this?'

Abraham looked at the ground, his face full of shame. He knew he had behaved badly. 'I said to myself, "There is surely no fear of God in this place, and they will kill me because of my wife," ' he said lamely. 'Besides,' he went on, 'she really is my sister, the daughter of my father though not of my mother; and she became my wife.' But Abraham knew his reply was inadequate.

Abimelech frowned and shook his head. He felt seriously wronged, but rather than cause trouble over the issue, he decided to settle it in a peaceful, honourable way. He sent for his servants and gave Abraham a huge gift of sheep, cattle and slaves, plus a thousand shekels and then added, 'My land is before you. Live wherever you like.' What more could he do?

Abraham still could not meet the king's gaze. He had failed. Again. Worse still, he had ended up being rebuked and taught a lesson in honesty from a man who did not even know God!

He sighed to himself. God had proved himself to be faithful, time and time again, but for his part he had learned little. He had not dealt with his fears or learned to trust God to protect him, and even after witnessing how seriously God treated sin at Sodom and Gomorrah, he still ended up sinning himself again.

He looked up hesitantly at Abimelech, feeling disgusted with himself. What could he say to the man? In the end he did the only thing he knew how to do. He went to the Lord God and prayed that Abimelech's household would be healed from barrenness. That was the least he could do. And in his mercy, God listened and answered.

The two men went their separate ways, both knowing their relationship had been breached, even before it had begun. Later, though, they had another chance to make it work. Abimelech was concerned about Abraham's influence and spiritual power and saw him as a threat. So the two men signed a treaty of friendship at Beersheba and the agreement held, even during a dispute over a well which could have turned into a full-scale war.

For his part, God knew that Abraham still needed to face

another test to cement his friendship. But this time it needed to be one he would never forget.

* * *

Abraham's deceit towards Abimelech must have been the lowest point of his life. He showed once again, somewhat surprisingly, that he was prepared to sacrifice Sarah's life to save his own. His fears obscured his integrity, his friendship with God and his love for his wife. It was a tragic incident, but one that can give us real encouragement as we try to develop our friendship with God.

It shows that God will be faithful to people who slip up from time to time. This does not give us a licence to sin, but it gives us confidence that he will take care of those who are normally loyal and obedient, but who get it wrong sometimes.

It also shows again the lengths God will go to to keep his people from adultery. He understands the seriousness of this sin far more than we ever will and sets boundaries of protection over our lives. It's a foolish person who ignores those boundaries or tries to break out of them. As Jude says (v.21), we all have to make a choice to keep ourselves in God's love.

Abraham gives hope to those of us who struggle with long-standing sin problems. We are not alone! He faced the same problems we do. He did not just battle with fear. In this situation he was also selfish, he lied and he showed a mistrust of God.

It is sad that Abraham carried this sin tendency for more than 30 years and did not get it dealt with. But when I look at my own life, I find I am pretty much the same. If we are honest, we all have areas of our lives that we know are wrong, but we cannot be bothered to confront them, so we leave them dormant, hoping they will go away. They never do, however, because there are no remedies apart from the cross and the blood of Jesus. Ignoring things never achieves anything.

Because God loves us, he will do what he did with Abraham and put us in a position where they are exposed, so they can be dealt with once and for all. It's painful when it happens, but we end up better for it and it develops our friendship with him further, for a true friend is someone who cares enough about us to want the very best for us, even if it means causing us a bit of pain to achieve it.

9

The Big Test

The woman's screams penetrated the stillness of the night –
repeated cries of agony. Then there was momentary silence,
followed by the rasping cry of a newborn baby. Abraham
rushed into the women's quarters of the tent, his face wreathed
in smiles. Several excited slave girls followed him, chattering
and squealing with delight. Abraham pulled back the curtain
and the maidservant who was the midwife in Abraham's clan
gestured for them to come in. Abraham peered through the
candlelight where his ageing wife was lying on the animal skin
bed, her face covered in sweat. She looked up at her husband
with delight and thrust the little bundle into his arms, tears
streaming down her face. Abraham cried too. Their years,
decades, of waiting were finally over. God had been faithful.
He had heard their cries, had seen their sorrow and had kept his
promise. As ever, his timing was immaculate.

Abraham cuddled his son fondly, and Sarah began to laugh.
But this time it was not the sneering, mocking laugh of a barren
woman. This was a laugh of joy, of happiness, of contentment.

'God has brought me laughter,' she said, scarcely able to get
the words out, 'and everyone who hears about this will laugh
with me.' She had a point. After all, she was well past child-

bearing age, and Abraham was 100. As her chuckling continued, Abraham joined in, and so did his servants, family and friends who were standing in the tent. There was no doubt about it – Isaac was well named. He was bringing them laughter already. Well, most of them. In his excitement, Abraham did not notice his 17-year-old son Ishmael sulking in the shadows, his face taut with resentment.

A few days later, the family gathered together again to witness the ritual of circumcision. Maybe Abraham was the only one who noticed the way the little baby laid perfectly still as he performed the messy ceremony. He did not wriggle or cry at all – he just laid there, offering no resistance. Afterwards the servants killed one of the best calves and roasted it for a special family feast. And what a feast it was! The singing, dancing, eating and drinking went on late into the night – a time of joyful family celebration. There was no doubt that God had taken Abraham and Sarah into a new season of joy.

Sadly, as in most families, the joy did not last for ever.

Three years later, it was time for Isaac to be weaned (babies in that Eastern culture were breast-fed for far longer than those in the West), and weaning was not just a natural stage of growing up. It was also a significant time spiritually, especially for the first-born son, for it meant that the baby was taking his rightful place as heir of the household. Another huge family feast marked the event.

Servants in Abraham's household had been preparing the celebration for a long time, and now the big moment had arrived. The best calves and sheep were roasting on the fires and tables were laden with fruit, vegetables and wine as Abraham led young Isaac out of the tent to the clapping and shrieks of family and friends. He was wearing a robe specially made for the occasion – a robe signifying Isaac as his father's heir. The party began. There was, however, one notable absentee: Ishmael. He had changed enormously since the birth of his half-brother. He had always been wild and rebellious but was more so now. There was constant conflict as he tried to come to terms with losing the undivided attention of the father he adored, as well as his position as the family heir. He was becoming an angry, jealous young man.

The celebration was more than he could cope with. The mere sight of Isaac wearing the robe made him boil with rage and in the end he could not contain himself any longer. As Abraham prayed for Isaac, he stood in the tent doorway, muttering insults and mocking his half-brother.

Sarah, who was always watchful when Ishmael was around, turned and glared at him. She had had enough. The resentment she used to feel towards Hagar boiled up again inside her and she turned to Abraham. 'Get rid of that slave woman and her son,' she said, her teeth gritted with anger. She could not even bear to say Hagar's name. 'For that slave woman's son will never share in the inheritance with my son Isaac.' She shook her head emphatically as she said the word 'never'. She clearly meant every word.

The atmosphere at the feast became charged with tension as Abraham tried to placate his angry wife. But the damage was done – the celebration had been ruined. Ishmael, sensing his father's concern, diplomatically removed himself from the scene rather than cause any more trouble. As the evening continued, Abraham grew more concerned. He could see where the situation was heading and yet could not contemplate banishing the son he loved so dearly. It would be the equivalent of sending the boy to his death; something that no responsible father could possibly consider. It went right against his natural instincts as a parent. And yet Sarah was right. Ishmael's presence in the household had become an increasing source of embarrassment since Isaac's birth. Servants and other family members were talking about it. It was a situation that was going to get worse.

Then God spoke to him about it, just at the right time. 'Do not be so distressed about the boy and your maidservant. Listen to whatever Sarah tells you, because it is through Isaac that your offspring will be reckoned. I will make the son of the maidservant into a nation also, because he is your offspring.'

Abraham immediately felt relieved. Although it would break his heart to send Ishmael away, he knew that he could cope now that God had reassured him. And having made the decision, it was best to act on it quickly. So early the next morning, just after sunrise, Abraham woke Ishmael and sent a servant to rouse Hagar. He had already gathered together some food, along with some water in the skin of a lamb, sewn up and ready to be carried by its legs over Hagar's shoulders. The supplies were not that plentiful, but Abraham thought that if they did not have a lot of food, they might end up living nearby so he could still keep in touch. He did not realise that Hagar had other ideas.

He called Ishmael over to him and embraced him, tears coursing down his wrinkled cheeks. Ishmael, tough as he was, was crying too. The father and son continued hugging one another for a long time until Hagar, her face set and determined, came and pulled Ishmael away. 'Come on, son,' she said. 'We have no place here.' Picking up the supplies, she turned abruptly and walked away, deliberately not even glancing at Abraham. Ishmael followed hesitantly, glancing back repeatedly at his father as they walked into the desert. And he kept on looking and waving until Abraham was just a tiny speck on the horizon.

Once they were out of sight, Abraham went into his tent and wept bitterly, the tears that only a parent who has lost a child will understand. Maybe he did not realise that he had in fact passed another test of obedience, which had deepened his friendship with God and prepared him for other trials that lay ahead.

He needn't have worried about the teenage boy who had been the apple of his eye for so long, for God kept his promises to Hagar and Ishmael. He saved their lives as they trudged through the wilderness, trying to get to the road that ran from central Palestine to Egypt and the safety of her own people. Abraham never saw his son again and took his pain to his grave. But God made Ishmael a great nation.

* * *

The dark sky gradually began to lighten and birds started to sing to herald a new day. Abraham was up already. Like most nomads, he always rose early to make the most of the cool temperatures. He was about to call a servant to bring him some water when he became aware of God's presence in his tent. It was some time since his friend the Lord had spoken to him. He had not visited him since the day he had told him to send Ishmael away, but he recognised the voice straight away and fell to his knees, waiting for God to speak to him.

'Take your son,' God said, 'your only son, Isaac, whom you love, and go to the region of Moriah. Sacrifice him there as a burnt offering on one of the mountains I will tell you about.'

God's presence ebbed away, leaving Abraham still kneeling, trying to cope with the words he had just heard. His mind was a turmoil of questions. Kill Isaac? How could he? And why would God demand such an offering when human sacrifices were abhorrent to him? What about God's promise to use Isaac to birth a great nation? How could that happen if Isaac were dead?

Abraham continued kneeling and gradually sensed peace come to his troubled mind. He thought about his friend, the

Lord, and the number of times he had promised him a son – a son who would produce descendants of his own. What was it he had said to him after he had left Melchizedek all those years ago? The words came back to him: 'A son coming from your own body will be your heir. Look up at the heavens and count the stars, if indeed you can count them. So shall your offspring be.' Those words, given to him in a vision, were reassuring. God had kept his word to Abraham, time after time, and would surely do so again. So Isaac would somehow be safe. Even if Abraham killed him, then God would bring him back to life again. Either that or God was a complete liar, and that could not possibly be the case.

Abraham rose to his feet, feeling more confident. His only option was to do as God said and trust him to keep his promises about Isaac. One thing was certain, however. There was no way he could tell Sarah or anybody else what God had said. They would never understand and would try to stop him doing God's will. He decided to keep God's instructions to himself.

The following day, Abraham rose early again, saddled his donkey and set off with Isaac and two of his servants. The animal was already loaded up with wood for the fire. The journey was around 30 miles and the men walked slowly in the typical fashion of desert-dwellers, who never rushed anywhere. Isaac wondered why his father seemed preoccupied. He sensed that this was no ordinary mission.

Two days later they arrived at a place just a few miles outside Jerusalem, a high promontory jutting into the Kidron Valley. Moriah was visible in the distance. Abraham stopped and scanned the horizon. His mouth was dry and his face tense as he told his servants, 'Stay here with the donkey while I and the boy go over there.' He gestured towards Moriah. 'We will worship and then we will come back to you.' The servants nodded and sat under the shade of some bushes to rest. They wondered why their master had hesitated slightly as he said '*we* will come back to you'.

Abraham picked up a long-bladed knife and a small brazier containing some smouldering coals, which he had lit earlier in the day. Then he gave Isaac the bundle of firewood and put his arm round his son as they walked slowly up a hill, a man well over 100 with his fully grown son. Neither of them spoke. Words did not seem necessary. Isaac sensed his father's tension but did not feel he could ask him what was on his mind. He simply drew closer to the dad he loved, somehow knowing that they needed to be together.

After a while they came to some woods, well out of view of the servants. Isaac broke the silence. 'Father?' he said tentatively.

'Yes, my son?' Abraham replied.

'The fire and the wood are here,' Isaac replied, 'but where is the lamb for the burnt offering?'

Abraham hesitated for a moment. He could not tell his son the truth. Not yet. 'God himself will provide the lamb for the burnt offering, my son,' he said affectionately, squeezing Isaac's shoulder.

The two of them continued walking up the hill and then Abraham stopped. He knew this was the place God had told him about. He looked around and saw some piles of rocks and stones. These would do. Abraham picked them up one at a time and built a rough altar, and took the wood and laid it on top. Then, with his hands shaking, he tied Isaac's hands and feet with some twine that he had brought with him, and laid him on the altar. He could barely bring himself to look at the son he loved so much. Memories of Ishmael flooded momentarily into his mind. How could he do this? He had exiled one son, and now he was killing another. What was he doing? He looked at Isaac, who was lying uncomfortably on the wood, and breathed in deeply to try and stop himself from crying. How could his son just lie there like this? Why didn't he fight him off? After all, he was fit and strong and could have easily wrestled his way out of the situation had he wanted to. Abraham fleetingly recalled how Isaac had laid there peacefully during his circumcision. He was doing the same again. The tears welled up in Abraham's eyes.

Resolutely he got his thoughts under control again, and seized the knife. Then, shutting his eyes, he drew it high in the air, ready to plunge it into Isaac's heart. His arm was just swinging down when a voice called from heaven urgently, loudly. 'Abraham! Abraham!'

He hesitated, the knife poised. He recognised the voice from before. It was the angel of the Lord. 'Here I am,' he replied.

'Do not lay a hand on the boy,' said the Lord. 'Now I know that you fear God because you have not withheld from me your son, your only son.'

Abraham sat down on the altar, perspiration pouring from his brow. He was shaking violently. He looked at Isaac and smiled, and then reached out and ruffled his hair before untying him. The two of them embraced one another fondly and were still doing so when a commotion caught their attention. A few yards away they noticed a ram, caught by its horns in a bush. Abraham went over, released it, slit its throat and then, with Isaac's help, dragged it onto the altar and set light to the wood.

Turning to his son he said, 'I think we should call this place Yahweh-yireh, The Lord Will Provide.' Isaac nodded hastily in agreement! Relief was still written over his face. The Lord had certainly provided a sacrifice in the most dramatic way. Then they looked to the sky as the angel of the Lord spoke to them from heaven again. It was the first time Isaac had heard God speak. 'I swear by myself', said the angel, 'that because you have done this and have not withheld your son, your only son, I will surely bless you and make your descendants as numerous as the stars in the sky and as the sand on the seashore. Your descendants will take possession of the cities of their enemies, and through your offspring all nations on earth will be blessed, because you have obeyed me.'

Abraham and Isaac stood gazing towards heaven for a long time, their arms around one another. After a while they embraced one another again.

'Let's go back to the servants,' said Abraham.

As they walked down the slope, away from the smouldering sacrifice, they knew that life would never be the same again.

Abraham had faced the ultimate test of his friendship with God. And he had passed.

* * *

There comes a moment in most of our lives when we face a supreme test of our commitment and devotion to God. It can come in a variety of forms, but it will invariably involve pain. Fortunately we never have to face these tests alone, and they are not tests as the world sees them, where everything hangs on whether we pass or fail. God is not sitting in heaven with a cosmic clipboard, totting up our marks. He is more concerned about what is in our hearts and what we learn about him and ourselves along the way. In fact the tests are more for our benefit than God's, since he knows our character anyway. His tests are to show us, and possibly other principalities and powers (Job 1:8), what we are like, especially in our friendship with him.

The only way to achieve real growth is through painful sacrifice. Abraham's life with God comprised a series of tests, culminating with the sacrifice of Isaac. He did well in some, but messed up badly in others.

When famine came to Canaan, he failed by not believing

God's promise to provide for him.

When faced with the prospect of losing his life so Sarai could become Pharaoh's wife, he failed again by resorting to lies and deceit.

When faced with a dispute with Lot over the division of pastures, he passed by giving Lot first choice.

When given the responsibility of rescuing Lot and other prisoners taken captive by Kedorlaomer, he passed by gaining a courageous victory.

When offered tempting gifts from the King of Sodom, he passed by turning them down.

In the situation regarding Sarai's barrenness, he failed by compromising and sleeping with Hagar.

He did better when given the test of interceding for his family and the city of Sodom.

But he resorted to lies and deceit again when King Abimelech tried to take Sarah into his household.

He did well when God commanded him to send Ishmael into exile. He complied, even though it must have broken his heart. And his success in this situation gave him essential preparation for the test involving Isaac. God often gives us rehearsals to equip us for difficult trials. It's all part of his training programme.

On this analysis, Abraham only passed around half the tests God set him – a success rate that you and I may well identify with. On most occasions when Abraham passed a test, God spoke to him afterwards. Many people say that God goes quiet during times of real trial, and this is often the case. This does not mean that he has left us, for his presence is very strong, but he tests our maturity in the silence, to see how we fare and then speaks to us when the test is over.

Abraham certainly passed the test that mattered: the one involving Isaac. His obedience demonstrated how he had grown over the years, and the fact that his friendship with God mattered more than anything. In this situation, God was trying to establish two things: whether Abraham's love for his Lord was greater than anything else; and whether he was looking to God himself to fulfil the promises for his life, rather than to Isaac.

Building a friendship with God

Much has been written over the years about that amazing day in Moriah. But there are several aspects that strike me as being particularly important in relation to building a friendship with God:

1. We should see God's tests as an honour

I used to moan terribly when I was going through hard times and blamed everybody else for them, including God. I still do sometimes. It's easy to have a negative attitude when things go wrong. Yet Peter, who knew what it was like to face trials, said, 'Do not be surprised at the painful trial you are suffering, as though something strange were happening to you. But rejoice that you participate in the sufferings of Christ, so that you may be overjoyed when his glory is revealed' (1 Peter 4:12).

One thing that strikes me about Abraham is that he never complained. I am sure he struggled, but he must have seen the difficulties as a privilege, as a way of deepening his relationship with God, and no doubt experienced the joy Peter referred to when God's glory was revealed in his life. We should try to do the same. Although God wants us to be honest with him about how we feel, he nevertheless regards grumbling as sin. We need to repent of it and gladly embrace the opportunities for growth and friendship provided by these tests, rather than moan about them.

2. God only gives us tests that we can handle

God will never put you through a trial that you cannot handle, so if you face a test, be encouraged – the only reason it has come your way is because God knows you are ready for it. You might not feel ready – in fact you might feel completely unequipped – but try to see it as God's way of showing you that your capacity is bigger than you thought. Look at it this way: the test is there and is not going to go away, so you can either sit and grumble about it and sink into depression, or you can reach out and find God's grace to get through it. God will always provide a way through his trials, but we have to be willing to seek it and find it.

God only asked Abraham to sacrifice Isaac because he knew he was ready to face a big challenge. It came after God had spent decades working on Abraham's character.

God has different tests for each of us and they often involve sacrificing the things that are dearest to us. It is his way of establishing correct priorities in our lives. Some parents are actually called to surrender the lives of their children – possibly the hardest test of all. My wife and I had to do it once. When our four-month-old baby was suffering from severe meningitis and had just hours to live, we stood by his bedside and offered him to the Lord, just as Abraham did with Isaac. Fortunately God spared his life, just as he did Isaac's, but there were no guarantees. We were not confident of getting him back.

All parents have to learn the painful lesson of sacrificing their children into God's providential care as they grow up. This can be desperately painful, especially if they do not follow God and maybe have rejected him. But it is the only way; the only way to show God that we really love him, and the only way to allow him to have his perfect way in their lives.

3. We should respond to God's instructions immediately

One phrase you sometimes come across during Scripture's account of Abraham's life is 'early the next morning'. It is used to describe how Abraham did God's will straight away. He did not dither, wait for a confirmation, or pray further about it. He heard and acted – every time. This unhesitating attitude was, I believe, one of the keys to Abraham's success. I sometimes wonder whether we procrastinate too much about obeying God. I think he would rather have people who obey him straight away, even if they make mistakes, than people who wait around and never actually achieve anything.

4. We need to be prepared to let our dreams die, unconditionally

God has given every one of us an Isaac – that dream, that promise, that ambition to do something great for him. Some people are born with their Isaac. Others discover it as they go on in their Christian faith. But it is always there. It is not any ordinary desire. It is something significant – the embodiment of our reason for being on earth, the same as Isaac was for Abraham.

But there comes a time when we must be prepared to let that dream die; to put it on the altar and kill it, with no guarantees that God will bring it back to life again. It is a desperately painful process, because it involves failure, and no one likes to fail. When we go through it, something inside us dies as well, and we have to be ready to face the biggest disappointment of our lives. But it is a crucial stage in the development of any dream or plan that we have for God, for it gives God a chance to show us whether that Isaac has become more important to us than he is. It tests our motivation and reveals whether or not we are prepared to love him, even if he appears to let us down.

The great thing is that God usually gives us back our Isaacs, as he did to Abraham, once he is sure that our motives are right. After a few months or even years, he will begin to fulfil that original dream in his own way. We will discover that we have become broken enough to cope with it.

Maybe you have seen your fondest dream die before your eyes. Don't be discouraged. God may have taken it from you as a sacrifice, but if you hold fast and don't become bitter, he may well give it back to you – and in a much greater way than you could have imagined.

5. *Abraham had learned to recognise his friend's voice*

Being able to recognise God's voice is vitally important for a Christian, because if we don't recognise him we will never be able to obey him. And yet it is one area that God's people struggle with. This is a surprise really, when most of us have got several thousand pages of God's word stuck on a shelf somewhere!

Being familiar with God's voice can make the difference between life and death. Imagine what would have happened had Abraham not realised it was God calling him when he was about to stab Isaac! Had he not recognised his Lord, or not bothered to listen, the result could have been fatal. But his recognition was immediate, because he had taken the time to get to know God over many years. This is why he was able to respond immediately, saying, 'Here I am.' He uses these three words twice in this chapter: first when God told him to sacrifice Isaac and then again when he told him to stop. They are words that were, I believe, one of the secrets of Abraham's faith. He was always on call.

Friendship with God means talking to him and listening to him. After all, it's quite hard to build a friendship with somebody if we never dialogue with them. So we all have a responsibility to spend time with God and recognise his voice better than anybody else's. If we don't, we could find ourselves in difficulty when we face trials in the future.

6. God rewards us when we pass a test

God always rewarded Abraham when he did well in a divine test. Sometimes the reward was hearing God speak to him. On other occasions God gave him even greater promises for his life. Another time he rewarded him for his intercession for Sodom by saving Lot. And the same principle applies to other people in Scripture. Few people were tested more than Job was. But once he came through, God doubled everything he had lost (Job 42:12–13). This is why James says, 'You have heard of Job's perseverance and have seen what the Lord finally brought about. The Lord is full of compassion and mercy' (James 5:11). If you are going through a testing time at the moment, try to keep your eye on the reward ahead. There will probably be one now, and God's compassion and mercy certainly guarantee one in heaven.

7. God's tests do actually stop!

Some Christians seem to face an unfair share of trials. They lurch from one test to the next without time to catch their breath. To be honest this gives me a problem, for they seem to be tested more than anybody in Scripture ever was. Abraham went years, decades even, without God testing him, and during these times he enjoyed peace and plenty. The devil only tested Jesus for a while, and then left him alone (Luke 4:13). If we are finding that nothing is working out in our lives and that the testing never seems to stop, we need to go to God and other people and ask why. But whatever you are pushing through right now, keep going. One day your tears of doubt and pain will turn to those of understanding and relief.

* * *

As Abraham returned to his clan a few days later, Sarah noticed he was different. She could not explain why and did not ask. There seemed to be a quiet reassurance about him; a peace she had never seen before. She guessed it was because he had met with God again.

Later, over a meal, he and Isaac told her about their encounter with God at Moriah. She cried as they described how close Isaac had been to death and went up and hugged him tight. Isaac and Abraham were both weeping too. They were tears of a family who had pushed through pain barriers to discover a real richness in their friendship with God.

Epilogue

The test that Abraham faced with Isaac was his last one. After that sobering day in Moriah, he spent his last 25 years doing what all elderly people should do: he enjoyed God's blessing. Genesis 24:1 says that God blessed him in every way during those final years, which was proof that Abraham's friendship with the Lord had reached a point where those blessings penetrated all areas of his life.

Of course, like many people, Abraham had family matters to deal with in his old age. Isaac needed a wife, and not any old wife, but a woman from among his own people. That had to be carefully arranged to ensure that God's promises would be fulfilled. And Abraham also did what some elderly folk do: he remarried after Sarah's death. His new wife was a lady named Keturah and God's blessing was on him to such an extent that he managed to produce another six children at the age of well over 100, which is food for thought! One of those six was a young man named Midian, whose descendants became bitter enemies of Isaac's.

Abraham lived long enough to see his grandchildren. He did not die until Jacob and Esau were around 15, and probably had to maintain a respectful silence, as all granddads do, when he saw Isaac make all kinds of mistakes rearing those feuding twins. And like most people who are approaching death, he made sure that details of his inheritance were sorted out so there would not be any arguments later.

His latter years were, of course, blighted by Sarah's death. He suffered agonies of grief. Genesis 23:2 tells us that he mourned and wept for her, and then found her a decent burial plot. He chose a cave in a field at Machpelah, near Mamre, the place where they had spent many years together. He paid for the site, even though it was part of the land God had already told him was his.

He died at the age of 175. He 'breathed his last and died at a good old age, an old man and full of years' (Genesis 25:8). There was a touching moment when Isaac and Ishmael came together to bury him alongside Sarah – probably the only time the two half-brothers found peace with one another. Many families reunite at funerals, sadly only to go back to war straight afterwards.

Genesis 25:8 tells us that Abraham was gathered to his people. He went home to see his friends: Adam, Eve, Enoch, Noah and many others too. And, of course, his best Friend, God.

The Lord had called round to Abraham's home several times. Now it was Abraham's turn to go to God's place. I think he would have felt at home there.

* * *

By faith Abraham, when called to go to a place he would later receive as his inheritance, obeyed and went, even though he did not know where he was going. By faith he made his home in the promised land like a stranger in a foreign country; he lived in tents, as did Isaac and Jacob, who were heirs with him of the same promise. For he was looking forward to the city with foundations, whose architect and builder is God.

By faith Abraham, even though he was past age – and Sarah herself was barren – was enabled to become a father because he considered him faithful who had made the promise. And so from this one man, and he as good as dead, came descendants as numerous as the stars in the sky and as countless as the sand on the seashore . . .

By faith Abraham, when God tested him, offered Isaac as a sacrifice. He who had received the promises was about to sacrifice his one and only son, even though God had said to him, 'It is through Isaac that your offspring will be reckoned.' Abraham reasoned that God could raise the dead, and figuratively speaking, he did receive Isaac back from death. (Hebrews 11:8–12, 17–19)

Study Guide

Chapter 1: A Friendship Begins

1. What excuses do you sometimes make for not living the kind of life God wants you to live?

2. Abram made huge sacrifices to go on with God. Discuss the things you have given up since you became a Christian. How difficult was it? Has it been worth it?

3. What are the things in your life that could cause you to settle down, or stop you from going the whole distance with God like Abram did?

Chapter 2: A Time of Promise

1. God called Abram to break away from his culture. What kind of hold does your culture have on you? How can you free yourself from unhealthy aspects of culture?

2. Are your family a help or a hindrance to your Christian growth? If they are a hindrance how can you deal with this and yet still love them?

3. Abram always obeyed God straight away. How easy do you find it to do this? Can you think of any examples where you have obeyed him immediately – and where you have not? Discuss the consequences of each example.

4. Name some of the promises that God has made over your life. How many of them have come to pass? And how many are you still waiting for?

Chapter 3: Exploring the Land

1. Abram faced enemies in his promised land. What are the enemies that you face in possessing your promised land? How can you deal with them more effectively?

2. Do you find change easy? If not, why? Discuss areas where God is calling you to change.

3. Some of Abram's actions were prophetic without him realising it. Is it possible for our actions to have the same significance? Give some examples from your own life.

Chapter 4: Failure and Compromise

1. Abram sometimes found that obeying God actually made things worse for him. Have you ever found the same? Discuss why a loving father would require you to take the difficult path in some situations.

2. Do you struggle to trust God with the everyday things in life like Abram did? What can we do to strengthen our faith in these areas?

3. Although Abram obeyed God, he also compromised in some areas. Why was that? Can you think of other people in Scripture who compromised? What were their reasons and what were the results?

4. Abram took advantage of God's grace and continued to sin after he had been forgiven. How can we learn from his mistakes and be sure not to keep committing the same sins over again?

Chapter 5: A Friendship Is Restored

1. Lot fell into sin because he was not honest with his own heart and played around with temptation. What would you have done if Abram had offered you the first choice of the land?

2. Abram was prepared to back down in his dispute with Lot, even though he was in the right. Why was this? What stops us from doing the same in similar situations?

3. How can you show love to some of your enemies at the moment in a practical way?

4. What were Abram's motives in rescuing Lot? Why did he bother? What would you have done in the same situation? What does all this tell us about family ties?

Chapter 6: A Covenant Relationship

1. Abram went to war when he had to, even though he was not a warrior. What are some of the things God is calling you to fight against at the moment?

2. What authority do we have in Jesus' name in spiritual warfare? How can we enforce it in given situations?

3. God called Abram by name when he was struggling. Can you think of times when he has shown you love in a very personal way?

4. None of us likes bad news. And yet God prepared Abram for difficult times ahead for him and his family. Why was this? Are we open enough to hearing God give us bad news?

Chapter 7: A Friendship Is Sealed

1. Conceiving Ishmael was a terrible mistake. Can you think of times when you have taken God's promises into your own hands? What were the consequences?

2. Name some of your best friends of ten years ago. What is your relationship with them now? What happened in between?

3. How does God show you his friendship? And how do you show him friendship?

4. In what ways has God circumcised your heart since you became a Christian?

Chapter 8: A Woman In Need

1. Why did God think it was so important to visit Sarah personally? Do you think he still does the same thing today?

2. Have you ever 'bargained' with God in prayer like Abraham did with Sodom and Gomorrah? What was the result?

3. Discuss some things that you could begin interceding for today.

4. Does our society deserve the same treatment as Sodom and Gomorrah received? How do you think God sees the situation?

Chapter 9: The Big Test

1. Why do you think Abraham lapsed back into sin when he lied to Abimelech? Why did he not learn from the past?

2. Was Abraham right to listen to Sarah and send Ishmael away? What would you have done in a similar situation?

3. What is the dearest thing in your life, apart from God? How hard would you find it to give it up?

4. What tests has God taken you through in your Christian life so far? How did you do – did you pass them or fail them? What lessons did you learn?

5. Are there any things in your life that you have allowed to die? What has happened as a result? What do you think God is saying about them now?

Index of Life Issues

Page numbers often mark the beginning of a topic that continues for several pages.

CHARACTER & CHARISMA SERIES

SARAH
MOTHER OF A NATION

—

—

WENDY
VIRGO